M. Leanne Lachman and
Deborah L. Brett

global demographics 2009

SHAPING REAL ESTATE'S FUTURE

Urban Land Institute

Recommended bibliographic listing:

Lachman, M. Leanne, and Deborah L. Brett. *Global Demographics 2009: Shaping Real Estate's Future.* Washington, D.C.: Urban Land Institute, 2009.

Urban Land Institute
1025 Thomas Jefferson Street, N.W.
Washington, D.C. 20007-5201

ISBN: 978-0-87420-123-9
ULI Catalog Number: G18

10 9 8 7 6 5 4 3 2 1
Printed in the United States of America.

About the Urban Land Institute

The mission of the Urban Land Institute is to provide leadership in the responsible use of land and in creating and sustaining thriving communities worldwide. ULI is committed to

» Bringing together leaders from across the fields of real estate and land use policy to exchange best practices and serve community needs;

» Fostering collaboration within and beyond ULI's membership through mentoring, dialogue, and problem solving;

» Exploring issues of urbanization, conservation, regeneration, land use, capital formation, and sustainable development;

» Advancing land use policies and design practices that respect the uniqueness of both built and natural environments;

» Sharing knowledge through education, applied research, publishing, and electronic media; and

» Sustaining a diverse global network of local practice and advisory efforts that address current and future challenges.

Established in 1936, the Institute today has more than 38,000 members worldwide, representing the entire spectrum of the land use and development disciplines. ULI relies heavily on the experience of its members. It is through member involvement and information resources that ULI has been able to set standards of excellence in development practice. The Institute has long been recognized as one of the world's most respected and widely quoted sources of objective information on urban planning, growth, and development.

The Authors

M. LEANNE LACHMAN is president of Lachman Associates, a real estate consulting firm serving private and institutional investors. She is also an executive-in-residence at Columbia University's Graduate Business School and serves on the boards of Liberty Property Trust and Lincoln National Corporation.

After an early career in market analysis with Real Estate Research Corporation, where she served as president and chief executive officer for eight years and initiated the *Emerging Trends in Real Estate* publication, Lachman moved into portfolio management for pension funds. She spent 13 years as a partner with Schroder Real Estate Associates, which was sold to Lend Lease Real Estate Investments, where she was head of Real Estate Strategies.

Lachman is widely published and is a frequent speaker. She is a ULI governor; is listed in *Who's Who in America, Who's Who in Finance and Industry,* and *The World Who's Who of Women;* and received the James Graaskamp Award for pragmatic real estate research in 1997 from the Pension Real Estate Association. She was awarded a B.A. from the University of Southern California and an M.A. from Claremont Graduate University.

DEBORAH L. BRETT is a real estate and planning consultant for a wide range of public and private organizations, providing project-related market analyses. Areas of specialization include development planning, commercial revitalization, market-rate and affordable housing, mixed-use projects, and transit-oriented development.

Brett formed Deborah L. Brett & Associates, based in Plainsboro, New Jersey, in 1993. She previously served as senior vice president and director of consulting services at Real Estate Research Corporation in Chicago. In her 18-year career there, she directed land use policy analyses for many government agencies and prepared development strategies and analyses for private clients.

Brett holds a master's degree in urban and regional planning from the University of Illinois at Urbana–Champaign. She is a longtime member of ULI and a frequent contributor to its publications, including *Real Estate Market Analysis: A Case Study Approach,* used by real estate and planning programs at many universities. Brett is also a charter member of the American Institute of Certified Planners and Lambda Alpha, the real estate and land economics honorary society. She teaches classes in residential and retail market analysis for Rutgers University's Bloustein School of Planning and Public Policy.

Project Staff

Rachelle L. Levitt
Executive Vice President, Global Information Group
Publisher

Dean Schwanke
Senior Vice President, Publications and Awards

James A. Mulligan
Managing Editor

Lise Lingo
Publications Professionals LLC
Manuscript Editor

Betsy VanBuskirk
Creative Director

John Hall
John Hall Design Group
Book Design and Production

Craig Chapman
Director, Publishing Operations

Contents

Preface | Why Demographics Matter

Demographics are the foundation of real estate decision making. Population, household, and income characteristics—and the direction of future trends—determine whether demand will exist for new housing or retail space, and household mobility suggests where that new space should be built. Growth in the labor force, as well as characteristics of its composition (age, education, skills, and mobility), strongly influence the success of office and industrial properties.

Tens of millions of households will be created worldwide over the next ten to 20 years. Many will be very poor, but growing percentages will demand the trappings of a middle-class lifestyle: improved shelter, personal services, branded consumer goods, furniture and housewares, and participation in entertainment and leisure activities, all of which generate demand for modern real estate.

Nearly everyone who will be making decisions about where to live, work, shop, and play in real estate for the next 20 years is alive now. We know a great deal about where they reside, their educational backgrounds, their family compositions, their incomes, whether or not they work, where they prefer to travel, and on and on. Consequently, we can anticipate future real estate needs.

Although population growth is not an absolute prerequisite for successful investment and development, it certainly helps to work with rather than against trends. However, even areas with minimal growth need residential units as new households are formed and as more people choose to live on their own—young and old. New technologies and ever-changing consumer preferences create replacement demand. Buildings are given new uses, are renovated, and are demolished. Thanks to the global communications revolution, the aspiring middle classes and the poor want what only the wealthy could obtain previously.

Meeting the demands of explosive, evolutionary growth requires sensitivity to urban form and sustainable designs—new communities that offer mixed uses, walkable environments, and access to jobs. The real estate implications of demographic changes around the world are enormous.

This ULI monograph is the second in a series that explores global demographic trends and their effects on real estate. The 2008 report provided an overview of regional population characteristics and future prospects, as well as in-depth coverage of worldwide aging, migration, urbanization, and tourism. The regional focus was on the Americas, with information on Latin America and the Caribbean as well as the United States and Canada. Chapter 1 of this 2009 edition provides an updated overview of international population growth trends, expands upon last year's analysis of the Americas, and provides new insights for Asia and Oceania. Chapters 2 to 4 focus on this year's key themes: labor force, education, and productivity; personal income, purchasing power, and poverty; and retailing. Each chapter concludes with a summary of implications for real estate. Chapter 5 looks more closely at demographic trends and prospects for Europe, while chapter 6 examines the Middle East and Africa.

M. Leanne Lachman
Deborah L. Brett
May 2009

Executive Summary

Investing where demographic demand is strong and deep is far more rewarding over time than investing in markets with little or no growth. Looking forward, the greatest urban population increases will occur in the world's three largest countries: China, India, and the United States. Africa, the Middle East, and Southeast and South Asia will be the globe's fastest growing regions; they all have burgeoning labor forces, high urbanization rates, and nearly unlimited need for residential and commercial space. Europe presents a stark contrast: it is the one region of the world that will experience population decline between now and 2030. Russia alone is losing 800,000 people a year (see chapter 5). Mature but still growing economies will offer attractive real estate investment and development prospects once the current recession subsides. In this context, think the United States, Canada, the United Kingdom, Ireland, Australia, and New Zealand.

Figure E-1 profiles the young, developing parts of the globe and the ever grayer developed world. It illustrates several of this year's demographic themes:

▸▸ The "haystack" profile in the righthand pyramid reflects the fact that, over the past 40 years, population growth has slowed in the developed countries of the world.

▸▸ Were it not for steady growth in the six Anglo-American countries cited above, the bottom third of the righthand pyramid would be much narrower. In all six, the growth stems from in-migrants and their children.

▸▸ The developed world's large workforce is aging rapidly (see chapter 2), while the young labor pools of the Middle East, Africa, and South Asia are expanding in daunting numbers, as portrayed by the width of the base in the lefthand pyramid (see chapter 6).

▸▸ Fertility rates have dropped globally—even in developing countries. As national economies improve and household incomes rise, fertility drops, children receive more education, and they find better jobs than their parents.

▸▸ Many developing nations are truly emerging markets, with expanding numbers of moderate- and middle-income households that generate enthusiastic consumer demand (see chapter 4).

▸▸ Population growth is highest in the poorest countries, and they have the most difficulty reversing a cycle of abject poverty—places like Yemen, Bangladesh, Haiti, Liberia, and Afghanistan.

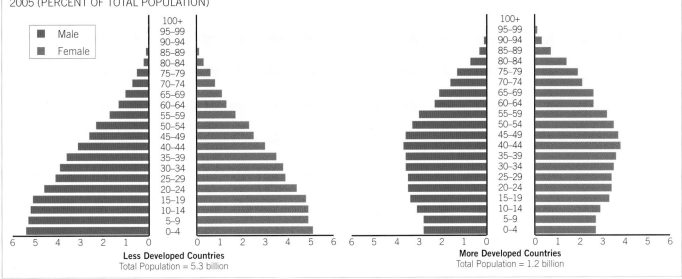

Population Pyramids: More Developed and Less Developed Countries
2005 (PERCENT OF TOTAL POPULATION)

Less Developed Countries
Total Population = 5.3 billion

More Developed Countries
Total Population = 1.2 billion

Source: UN Population Division, *World Population Prospects: The 2006 Revision*, http://esa.un.org/unpp.

▸▸ Aging was a key theme of 2008's *Global Demographics* report. The large cohorts in the upper portion of the righthand pyramid reflect the large older populations in Europe, Japan, and Northern America. In developing countries, the number of elderly is rising because of longevity gains, but their share of the total population is reduced by very large younger cohorts.

Europe

Population and labor force declines in Europe portend shrinking demand for real estate and suggest that development opportunities will be limited to the replacement of obsolete housing, retail, and office space. Population losses will not be uniform across Europe; in fact, the United Kingdom, Scandinavia, Ireland, France, Switzerland, and the Netherlands will continue to grow over the next 20 years. Urbanization and migration within countries will also generate demand: some cities will thrive, with vibrant office, retail, and entertainment cores, while others will contract.

Overall, though, Europe's need will be for replacement buildings, so the demolition of older properties will have to match new construction volumes. Without net new demand, supply cannot be expanded—or vacancies will rise, rents will fall, and values will decline. It will take a long time for domestic and foreign investors in Europe to grasp the extent to which negative population and labor force growth affect real estate occupancy and appreciation—or lack thereof.

Middle East and North Africa (MENA)

In direct contrast, a high proportion of the world's construction cranes have recently been located in the Middle East, with 20 percent said to have been in Dubai alone in the summer of 2008. The combination of population growth, urbanization, and oil revenues generate enough actual and potential projects to keep global architects and construction contractors busy. In a few locations, Dubai being most obvious, exuberance got out of hand;

however, most current residential and commercial development in MENA (from Egypt westward to Morocco) legitimately serves emerging regional economies.

As highlighted in chapter 6, the potential for real estate development in MENA is exemplified by Morocco and Turkey. By sending workers to Europe for generations, both have cultivated interchange with countries outside their regions. Turkey is further along the contemporary development spectrum, but Morocco was an intriguing destination long before Churchill and Roosevelt met in Casablanca in 1943. According to the World Bank, Turkey is already an upper-middle-income country, and Morocco is moving in that direction.

Sub-Saharan Africa

Because of their rapidly rising numbers, Africa's young people need to capture more of the world's work. When commodity demand picks up again, global attention will return to Africa. Anxious to secure copper, iron ore, oil, natural gas, uranium, and other resources, China is an active player now and, as a tradeoff, invests in infrastructure projects and assists mineral-rich sub-Saharan nations with economic development. Not to be outdone, India has begun the same process, emphasizing the long trading history between the continents and pointing to the 2 million ethnic Indians residing in Africa.

Labor and Real Estate

Because underlying economic growth is essential for strong property appreciation, the size and capabilities of national labor forces—as discussed in chapter 2—are important investment considerations. Growing numbers of moderate- and middle-income households generate demand for retail, residential, and hospitality projects; service employment growth supports office development; and industrial expansion requires manufacturing and distribution facilities.

America's real estate industry has two labor gaps, one visible now and one emerging:

▸▸ The skilled construction trades are not attracting enough young people: carpenters, sheet metal workers, electricians, mechanics, operating engineers, etc. Young people born in the United States are not being encouraged to work with their hands, so technical schools target new immigrants. This aspect of secondary and tertiary education deserves more focus.

▸▸ As baby boomers begin to retire, the industry will lose management talent. The succeeding demographic group—Generation X—tended to bypass real estate because there were no entry-level jobs when they finished college during the collapse in the early 1990s. Thus, the real estate industry lost a generation.

Emerging Moderate- and Middle-Income Households

Even in nations with a large percentage of low-wage workers or high income inequality, recent economic growth and changing demographics have resulted in the growth of middle-class and affluent households. As explained in chapter 3, middle-class gains occurred in nations as diverse as South Africa, Mexico, Ireland, and Poland. In China, greater affluence was spurred by new manufacturing jobs; in India, information technology creates white-collar and clerical job opportunities. In some countries, household incomes rise as remittances are sent home by relatives earning good wages abroad. Growing exports of oil and other natural resources are improving standards of living in nations throughout the Middle East, in Venezuela, and in parts of Africa.

As incomes improve in the developing world, moderate-income households can upgrade their shelter, move to permanent structures (with a lease or a mortgage), add more space, and enjoy safe drinking water and electricity. When poor families expand their buying power, demand increases for modern stores and shopping centers; successful entrepreneurs move from local informal markets into shop spaces. Employment grows along the way.

Global Retailing

Retail is the land use featured in this 2009 edition. As summarized in chapter 4, retailers will continue to seek cross-border locations, trying to find underserved and growing markets:

▸▸ For mid-price goods, they look to countries offering opportunities for critical mass.

▸▸ Emerging economies that are able to maintain positive growth in gross domestic product (GDP) in today's difficult environment—even in the 1 to 2 percent range—will be attractive to retailers that are facing stalled sales in their existing markets.

▸▸ Teenagers and young adults remain a targeted demographic for expanding specialty stores.

▸▸ The Internet poses an ever-increasing challenge to traditional brick-and-mortar stores, and not only in the world's richer countries. Online sales will suffer during the recession, but the pain will be milder than at mall shops.

▸▸ The credit crunch has made it impossible for developers in the United States, Canada, Europe, and Japan to start new projects, even if they have stable, committed tenants.

▸▸ Owners of good properties in top locations are focusing on retenanting any empty spaces and doing modest renovations to keep their centers attractive.

In the United States, the recession and the rise of Generation Y as consumers will shape the retail landscape:

▸▸ Successful chains will slow expansion plans as customers battle unemployment and adopt more frugal buying habits.

▸▸ Discount grocers will capitalize on their recent sales surge by expanding to new metropolitan areas. In centers with empty big-box spaces, they may be willing to take over 20,000 to 25,000 square feet—but they won't pay much.

▸▸ Although Generation Y shoppers grew up at malls, they rebel against seeing the same brands and the same designs throughout a center. Retailers have to address this issue and retain these shoppers, because baby boomers and retirees don't need more "stuff."

▸▸ By 2010, Generation Y will be larger than the baby boom generation—and will keep expanding as young adult immigrants enter the country. This huge generation will shape America as workers, consumers, parents, travelers, renters, and homebuyers (see chapter 1).

Barcelona, Spain.

Population Patterns | 1

Demographic megatrends and their expected regional variations over the next 20 to 40 years open this chapter. Then, because urbanization and population migration to cities will generate so much new real estate demand and because the United Nations has published new urban projections, this topic is featured. Finally, four geographic regions are reviewed in summary fashion: Northern America,[1] Latin America and the Caribbean, Asia, and Oceania.

The three regions featured in this 2009 edition—Europe, the Middle East and North Africa (MENA), and sub-Saharan Africa—are discussed in chapters 5 and 6, and appendix 2 contains country-by-country demographic data for those regions. In three thematic chapters—on labor; consumer income, poverty, and debt; and retail—the featured regions receive special attention, though all the subjects have global application.

Regional Population Growth

Earth's population of 6.7 billion will reach 8.3 billion by 2030 and 9.2 billion by 2050. As reflected across the bottom of figure 1-1, developed countries will contain a smaller and smaller share of the world's residents.[2] In truth, this category includes both growing and shrinking countries: Japan, the countries of the European Union, and Russia face population

Figure 1-1

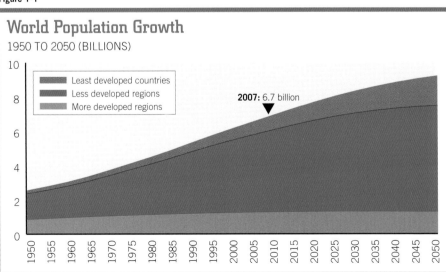

World Population Growth
1950 TO 2050 (BILLIONS)

Legend:
- Least developed countries
- Less developed regions
- More developed regions

2007: 6.7 billion

Source: UN Population Division, *World Urbanization Prospects: The 2007 Revision.*

declines, while six English-speaking countries that encourage immigration and assimilation of newcomers will continue to expand—the United States, Canada, the United Kingdom, Ireland, Australia, and New Zealand. Even so, the vast majority of global population growth is occurring in South Central and Southeast Asia, Africa, and the Middle East,[3] which all have burgeoning labor forces that are willing to work hard. The band at the top of figure 1-1 portrays the least developed countries,[4] which account for an increasing share of population growth. Unfortunately, poverty and high fertility tend to go together; and as fertility rates fall significantly in emerging markets, the least developed areas assume a higher percentage of total population increases.

Although mature economies, and particularly growing ones, offer attractive real estate investment and development prospects, emerging markets present nearly infinite opportunities to create residential, retail, office, logistics, and hotel properties, as well as master planned communities, to serve their growing populations. More basically, those nations also need infrastructure investment to literally pave the way for contemporary real estate development.

Figure 1-2 illustrates where growth will and will not occur over the next 20 years. As discussed in detail in chapter 5, Europe stands out as the one region experiencing population declines between now and 2030, with Russia alone losing over a million people per year. Europe's loss will be picked up fully by MENA and sub-Saharan Africa, as covered in chapter 6; these two regions will account for one-third of global growth. The

Figure 1-2

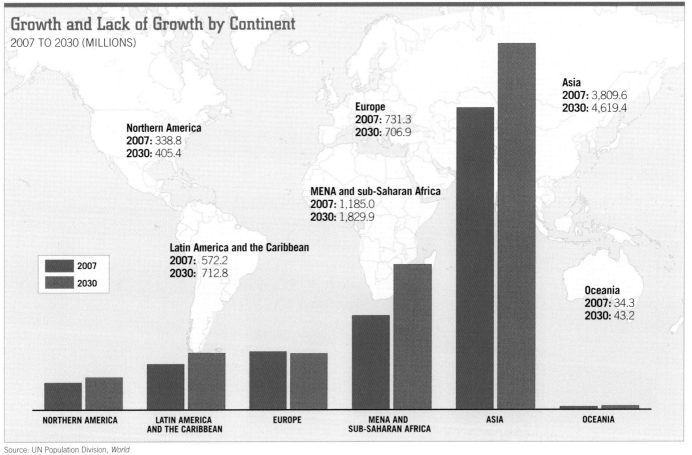

Growth and Lack of Growth by Continent
2007 TO 2030 (MILLIONS)

Northern America
2007: 338.8
2030: 405.4

Europe
2007: 731.3
2030: 706.9

Asia
2007: 3,809.6
2030: 4,619.4

MENA and sub-Saharan Africa
2007: 1,185.0
2030: 1,829.9

Latin America and the Caribbean
2007: 572.2
2030: 712.8

2007
2030

Oceania
2007: 34.3
2030: 43.2

NORTHERN AMERICA   LATIN AMERICA AND THE CARIBBEAN   EUROPE   MENA AND SUB-SAHARAN AFRICA   ASIA   OCEANIA

Source: UN Population Division, *World Urbanization Prospects: The 2007 Revision.*

Americas and Oceania will retain their proportional shares of global residents, as will Asia—with the difference being that far more people (six of every ten) will live on the vast Asian continent. Its demography is not uniform: the eastern area is growing slowly because of China's one-child policy and Japan's and South Korea's declining populations; whereas populations in huge countries in the south—like India, Pakistan, Bangladesh, and Indonesia—are mushrooming.

Reinforcing the regional population profile is figure 1-3's list of the 20 languages spoken most widely around the world. Mandarin Chinese is far and away the most pervasive, with an estimated 873 million native speakers and over a billion people able to converse in it. Hindi ranks a distant second, with 370 million native speakers but a total of almost 500 million people who can communicate in it, followed by Spanish (350 million), and then English with 340 million native speakers (but an estimated total of 510 million speakers, which puts it second only to Mandarin Chinese). Fifth and sixth on the list are Arabic and Portuguese, with Bengali a close seventh.

Urban Expansion

Ongoing urbanization generates massive demand for real estate around the globe. As illustrated in figure 1-4, the United Nations anticipates that the world's urban population will rise from 3.3 billion in 2007 to 6.4 billion in 2050, so this is not a short-term phenomenon. According to the UN Population Division, "The urban areas of the world are expected to absorb all the population growth over the next four decades."[5]

In most countries, natural increase (births over deaths) accounts for more urban growth than migration from rural to urban areas, though movement among cities is accelerating, typically from smaller urban areas to larger ones. Speaking of urbanization in the developing world, UN Habitat observers conclude that

> For every 60 million new urban dwellers added every year to the cities of the global
> South, approximately 36 million are born there, 12 million migrate in, and the
> remaining 12 million become urban residents by virtue of the reclassification of their
> rural lands to urban areas.[6]

A historical first occurred in 2008 when urbanites accounted for 50 percent of global residents. Henceforth, expect strong urban growth in most regions. Africa's urban population will treble between 2007 and 2050, and Asia's will double. The Americas will experience a gain of roughly 50 percent, whereas urban growth will be more modest in Oceania and Europe. By 2050, seven of ten global residents will live in urban areas, as compared with five of ten today. Within ten years, the world's rural population will begin to decline—to the point that 600 million fewer people will live in rural areas by 2050.

Urbanization in more developed regions of the world will rise from 74 percent today to as high as 86 percent by 2050. The Americas are already more than 80 percent urbanized but that figure will go up another ten percentage points by mid-century. Less developed regions will experience more explosive change, moving from 44 percent urbanized today to a probable two-thirds by 2050. As a driver of real estate demand,

Figure 1-3

The World's Top 20 Languages
(MILLIONS OF SPEAKERS)

Language	Native	Total
Mandarin Chinese	873	1,051
Hindi	370	490
Spanish	350	420
English	340	510
Arabic	206	230
Portugese	203	213
Bengali	196	215
Russian	145	255
Japanese	126	127
German	101	229
Punjabi	88	—
Javanese	76	—
Korean	71	—
Vietnamese	70	86
Telugu	70	75
Marathi	68	71
Tamil	68	77
French	67	130
Urdu	61	104
Italian	61	—

— = not available

Source: *Ethnologue:
Languages of the World, 2005.*

Figure 1-4

The World's Urban and Rural Populations
1950 TO 2050 (BILLIONS)

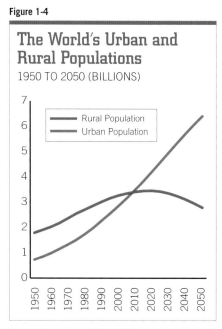

Source: UN Population Division, *World
Urbanization Prospects: The 2007 Revision.*

urbanization will be important in all growing countries; but the pressure in emerging markets will verge on overwhelming.

Not surprisingly, the greatest urban population increases will occur in the world's two dominant countries in terms of population size: China and India. Of the 1.3 billion urban residents to be added between now and 2025, 261 million will be in China and 197 million in India; together, the two countries will accommodate 35 percent of urban growth. From 2025 to 2050, the number of global urbanites will expand by another 1.8 billion; and again, one-third will be in India and China, but India's increase will be almost twice as large as China's. By mid-century, China's overall growth will be far slower.

Urbanization generates continuous demand for additional housing because each household migrating from a rural area needs a new city dwelling. Demand is deepest for low-cost units; but inmigrants exert pressure throughout a city's residential stock, and construction of moderate- and middle-income homes frees up older, existing units for households that cannot afford brand-new residences.

Inmigrants also need retail goods—from basic foodstuffs to furniture to alarm clocks— as well as health and education facilities. In all expanding areas, but particularly in rapidly urbanizing emerging markets, the continuing challenge is the expansion of infrastructure: water and sewer, transportation, electrification, schools, ports, jails, etc.

In the developing world, rural migrants tend to go first to small towns. Later, they or their descendants may move on to medium-sized cities, and subsequent generations might

Figure 1-5

Megacities in 2007 and 2025

2007		Rank	2025	
Urban Agglomeration	Population (Millions)		Urban Agglomeration	Population (Millions)
Tokyo	35.7	1	Tokyo	36.4
New York	19.0	2	Mumbai	26.4
Mexico City	19.0	3	Delhi	22.5
Mumbai	19.0	4	Dhaka	22.0
São Paolo	18.8	5	São Paolo	21.4
Delhi	15.9	6	Mexico City	21.0
Shanghai	15.0	7	New York	20.6
Kolkata	14.8	8	Kolkata	20.6
Dhaka	13.5	9	Shanghai	19.4
Buenos Aires	12.8	10	Karachi	19.1
Los Angeles	12.5	11	Kinshasa*	16.8
Karachi	12.1	12	Lagos*	15.8
Cairo	11.9	13	Cairo	15.6
Rio de Janeiro	11.7	14	Manila	14.8
Osaka-Kobe	11.3	15	Beijing	14.5
Beijing	11.1	16	Buenos Aires	13.8
Manila	11.1	17	Los Angeles	13.7
Moscow	10.5	18	Rio de Janeiro	13.4
Istanbul	10.1	19	Jakarta*	12.4
		20	Istanbul	12.1
		21	Guangzhou*	11.8
		22	Osaka-Kobe	11.4
		23	Moscow	10.5
		24	Lahore*	10.5
		25	Shenzen*	10.2
		26	Chennai*	10.1
*new additions		27	Paris*	10.0

Source: UN Population Division, *World Urbanization Prospects: The 2007 Revision.*

migrate to megacities. This pattern of graduated urbanization produces much faster growth rates in urban areas with fewer than 500,000 residents than in the world's biggest cities. In fact, half of urban growth between now and 2025 will be accommodated in small urban centers. The number of cities with 500,000 to 1 million residents will increase from 446 in 2005 to 551 in 2025. Even more extreme growth will occur among medium-sized cities with populations of 1 to 5 million: from 361 such cities in 2005 to 524 in 2025. In 2007, the world contained 30 large cities with 5 to 10 million inhabitants; by 2025, the number will be 48, three-quarters of which will be in developing countries.

The final urban category—a megacity—is an agglomeration with a minimum of 10 million residents. Today's 19 megacities are listed in figure 1-5, along with the eight to be added by 2025. By then, about 10 percent of the earth's urban population will live in these conurbations. Sixteen of the 27 will be in Asia, four in Latin America, three in Africa, and two each in Northern America and Europe.

For perspective, only two megacities existed back in 1950: New York, with a population of 12.3 million, and Tokyo, with 11.3 million. By 1975, Mexico City moved past the 10 million resident mark and became the world's third megacity. Between 1975 and 2007, 16 more agglomerations qualified. With one economy after another driven by global trade—in manufactured goods; in raw materials and commodities; in information technology, financial, and other services—big cities are where the action is and where upwardly mobile people aspire to live and work.

DEMAND FOR DEVELOPMENT

According to Abha Joshi-Ghani, manager of the World Bank's Urban Group, "Rapid urbanization is expected to increase the built areas in cities by 30 percent,"[7] generating incredible real estate development potential. Even though much initial demand in the developing world will be satisfied in slums, globalizing economies need manufacturing and distribution facilities, retail centers, hotels, offices, and housing for moderate-, middle-, and upper-income households.

Quantitatively, the deepest potential is in megacities, but they also have the most intense competition. Given the higher proportion of total growth occurring in cities with 1 to 10 million residents, those secondary and tertiary urban areas will need active developers. In Mexico, as an example, Homex—the large producer of affordable housing—spent many successful years concentrating outside the capital before expanding into Mexico City.

At higher price points, demand in secondary markets tends to be thinner. Hines Interests is currently active in Monterrey. Mexico's third largest city has just under 4 million people and, as home base for many of the country's largest companies, is quite affluent. Hines' residential projects target either middle-income or wealthy purchasers. For the latter, their Retama development represents the city's first high-end, vertical condominium complex. Four 17-story towers will eventually contain about 265 residences. Once complete, their project will probably have satisfied most local demand at that scale and price point. Hines currently enjoys a monopoly position in Monterrey's luxury high-rise market, but demand is too thin to replicate the project; Mexico City could absorb numerous such developments, but there would be price competition.

"Population growth is . . . largely an urban phenomenon concentrated in the developing world."

—United Nations, *World Urbanization Prospects: The 2007 Revision*

Figure 1-6

Urban Population Residing in Low-Elevation Coastal Zones
(PERCENT)

Asia	18.2
Oceania	14.3
MENA	12.6
Sub-Saharan Africa	8.7
Northern America	8.4
Europe	7.9
Latin America and the Caribbean	7.7

Source: UN Habitat, *State of the World's Cities, 2008/2009.*

WATER PROBLEMS

Provision and maintenance of infrastructure challenges all rapidly growing urban areas, but water is often a particularly worrisome issue. Coastal flooding threatens some large cities and will become more dangerous as sea levels rise. Salinity may also penetrate the water table and make well water undrinkable. Coastal cities are not the only ones with freshwater problems: supplies are inadequate in one major market after another—from Las Vegas to New Delhi.

Agriculture accounts for two-thirds of the world's freshwater consumption. As incomes rise in emerging markets and households begin to eat more meat, the water requirement for food production increases exponentially: ten times as much water is needed to produce one calorie from meat as is required to generate one calorie from a plant. Because so many of today's agricultural methods waste water, governments and agrarian companies are focused on efficient irrigation and sustainable food production.

Remediation in flood-prone urban locations is a daunting task. Reporting on recent work by the Organisation for Economic Co-operation and Development, UN Habitat authors state

The populations of Mumbai, Guangzhou, Shanghai, Miami, Ho Chi Minh City, New York City, Osaka-Kobe, Alexandria, and New Orleans will be most exposed to surge-induced flooding in the event of sea level rise. By 2070, urban populations in cities in river deltas, which already experience high risk of flooding, such as Dhaka, Kolkata, Rangoon, and Hai Phong, will join the group of most exposed populations.[8]

An acronym we will see more and more is LECZ (low-elevation coastal zones)—areas less than 10 meters (or 33 feet) above sea level. Although LECZ zones constitute only 2 percent of the earth's land area, they are home to 10 percent of the global population and 13 percent of urban dwellers.[9] As shown in figure 1-6, every region is affected but the highest percentages of threatened urbanites are in Asia, Oceania, and MENA. Apart from Venice's periodic *aqua alta*, one of the most extreme examples is in the tiny Micronesian nation of Kiribati, which is severely threatened by the rising Pacific Ocean. As salt gradually pollutes the groundwater, islands become uninhabitable long before they are actually submerged. Over time, Kiribati's population is being restricted to fewer and fewer islands.

Numerically, Asia's population is at greatest risk, with more than 250 million people living in LECZ urban areas, some of which are growing rapidly. One of the most vulnerable is Dhaka, the capital of Bangladesh, whose population of 13.5 million is expected to reach at least 22 million by 2025. Dhaka's elevation ranges from 2 to 13 meters above sea level. Almost 60 percent of the city's extremely dense slums have poor or no drainage and are already susceptible to frequent flooding.

Income, Rising Affluence, and Poverty

The World Bank classifies countries from low to high income on the basis of their per capita gross national income (GNI). Sub-Saharan Africa contains a concentration of poor nations, as will be illustrated in figure 3-1, but the low-income group also includes Pakistan, Afghanistan, Bangladesh, Cambodia, and Vietnam. Haiti is the only low-income country in the Western Hemisphere.

At the other end of the spectrum, high-income nations include the United States, Japan, South Korea, Australia, New Zealand, and most of western and northern Europe. This category also encompasses a number of small Caribbean islands with affluent expatriate populations, several Persian Gulf countries, and Estonia and the Czech Republic. The upper-middle-income cluster features a handful of African nations that have stable governments and well-developed economies (South Africa, Botswana, and Gabon), along with such other emerging markets as Russia, Romania, Turkey, Mexico, Argentina, and Brazil.

These classifications are helpful in identifying nations that warrant consideration for real estate investment. One caution, however: national, per capita averages often mask skewed distributions of household income, especially in countries with a small number of very wealthy families and millions of struggling low-income people. For years, Latin America exhibited that kind of inequality, but the situation is evolving as education becomes more pervasive and as more jobs are created in the formal sector. This topic is discussed further in the Latin America section of this chapter and again in chapter 3.

Poverty rates are falling worldwide, though progress is uneven. The number of poor individuals in sub-Saharan Africa, for example, rose by 30 percent between 1990 and 2005, but the proportion of people with incomes of less than $1.25 per day declined from 58 percent to 51 percent. More significant improvement was seen in South Asia, where the share of residents living on $1.25 a day or less fell from 52 percent in 1990 to 40 percent by 2005; these income gains happened while the overall population was increasing. In East Asia and the islands of Oceania, the proportion of people living on no more than $1.25 per day dropped from 55 percent in 1990 to less than 17 percent in 2005.

Figure 1-7 illustrates the proportion of the world's population living below various poverty levels. Using the standard of $1.25 per day, the poverty rate is less than 22 percent—though that still encompasses nearly 1.4 billion people. Given the worldwide recession, rates of poverty are undoubtedly moving up again. The countries in which more than half the population subsists on less than $1.25 per day are almost all in the eastern and western areas of sub-Saharan Africa.

The World Bank is now using a $2 per day standard to measure extreme poverty in Latin America and the Caribbean and in MENA because overall standards of living have risen considerably in both those regions. Using the $2 measure, about one in five people in each of these regions is extremely poor. Applying the $2 standard globally, two of every five persons are living in poverty.

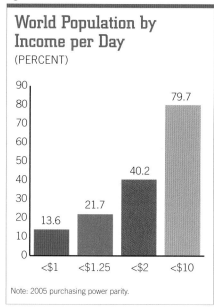

Figure 1-7

World Population by Income per Day
(PERCENT)

Note: 2005 purchasing power parity.

Source: World Bank, 2008
World Development Indicators.

Figure 1-8

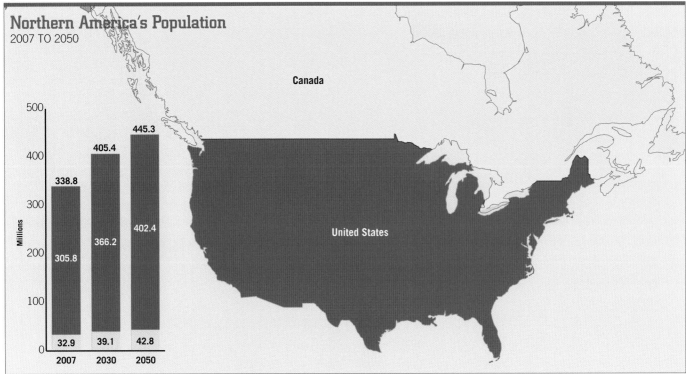

Northern America's Population
2007 TO 2050

Canada

United States

Millions

	2007	2030	2050

445.3
405.4
338.8
402.4
366.2
305.8
32.9 39.1 42.8

Source: UN Population Division,
*World Urbanization Prospects: The
2007 Revision*, tables A.1 and A.5.
http://esa.un.org/unup.

Global Regions

The 2008 edition of *Global Demographics* featured the Americas. This year's report pro-vides updated information on population trends in its subregions, as well as those in Asia and Oceania.

NORTHERN AMERICA

Consisting of the United States, Canada, Bermuda, and Greenland, Northern America contains 5 percent of global population. Between now and 2030, as shown in figure 1-8, 67 million people will be added, representing 4 percent of world growth. Northern America is the most urbanized region, with Bermuda at 100 percent, the United States at 81.4 percent, and Canada at 80.3 percent. As portrayed in figure 1-9, the movement of people from rural to urban areas is ongoing; by 2050, more than 90 percent of the region's popu-lation will live in cities and suburbs. As is true in all regions, migration to urban areas in Northern America generates real estate demand in receiving locations. Conversely, though, as populations fall in some less attractive urban areas, fewer residential and commercial buildings are needed and demolition is needed. Excess space becomes more visible in times of economic stress, and abandonment is now increasingly evident in the least appealing neighborhoods of low-growth or no-growth urban areas.

RETIREMENT—OR NOT? The oldest U.S. baby boomers are now 63 years old. Retirements have begun among this 78-million-person generation, but the recent financial collapse will delay full retirement for many workers in both Canada and the United States. For half a century, commentators have fixated on the predilections of the baby boomers, often convincing themselves that this demographic cohort was monolithic—despite the fact that their births extended over 18 years. If truth be told, the youngest boomers turned only 45 on January 1, and they have ample time to recoup their investments before retirement. The McKinsey Global Institute points out that the earnings peak for the oldest half of the baby boomers will occur in 2015; for the younger half, the peak will not be until 2025. Boomers have lots of working time ahead.[10]

According to an AARP survey conducted a year ago, 14 percent of retirees were considering returning to work because of stock market losses, and the proportion is surely higher now. For boomers approaching retirement age, this is a time of reconsideration. Although surveys have consistently shown that average baby boomers intend to work longer and more intensely past age 65 than their predecessors did, researchers have never been sure what would happen when the respondents actually reached retirement age. The results are now emerging:

▸▸ In early 2008, about 30 percent of 65- to 69-year-olds (pre-boomers) were either employed or looking for work, according to the Bureau of Labor Statistics. This is up from 24 percent in 2000. Among 60- to 64-year-olds, 54 percent were in the labor force, again up considerably from 47 percent in 2000.

▸▸ Government workers and union members with assured pensions tend to retire as soon as they can.

▸▸ Manual laborers, whose muscles wear out, prefer to retire when possible.

▸▸ Because white-collar jobs are less taxing physically, workers can continue well past 65, and many are doing so for both social and financial reasons. However, much of corporate America has not yet adapted to the concept and does not permit flexible or shorter hours.

▸▸ A lot of seniors are discovering second or third careers and launching new businesses, consulting, downshifting to lower-stress jobs, and combining volunteer and paid activities.

From 1970 to 2000, America's median retirement age dropped by about two years—to 62.6 years. For the sake of the labor market and for the financial well-being of new retirees, the nation needs to return to a median retirement age of 64 or 65 years, reinvent retirement, and create a more flexible labor market. If any group can pull that off, it will be the boomers; and the troubled economy may be the perfect catalyst.

The McKinsey Global Institute estimates that two-thirds of the early boomers (now 54 to 63 years of age) are financially unprepared for retirement.[11] When its report came out a year ago, the Institute thought many of these preretirees did not realize what financial shape they were in. Given the subsequent market decline, it seems safe to assume that the light has dawned.

GENERATION Y Not only are the boomers more diverse than frequently suggested, but they are not the only large demographic cohort. Generation Y or the 'Net generation, which contains 15- to 32-year-olds, totals 74 million.[12] As young adult immigrants arrive, they add to the ranks of this demographic group, so it will exceed the size of the boomer group next year and then keep growing.

Figure 1-9

Urbanization in Northern America
2007 TO 2050

	PERCENTAGE URBANIZED		
	2007	**2030**	**2050**
United States	81.4	87.0	90.4
Canada	80.3	84.0	87.9
Total Region	81.3	86.7	90.2

Source: UN Population Division, *World Urbanization Prospects: The 2007 Revision*, tables A.1 and A.2. http://esa.un.org/unup.

America's Working Artists

» Two million Americans' primary employment is as an artist.

» Another 300,000 claim secondary employment as artists.

» Half of all artists live in 30 metropolitan areas, and more than 20 percent are in one of five locations: Los Angeles, New York, Chicago, Washington, D.C., and Boston.

» Fifty-five percent of artists have college degrees—twice as high as in the overall labor force.

» More than one in three artists is self-employed versus 10 percent of the labor force.

» Artists generally earn less than workers with similar educations. At $15,000 per year, dancers have the lowest median income.

Artists' Occupations

2003–2005

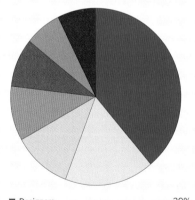

■ Designers..39%
▨ Performing artists.................................. 17%
▨ Fine artists, art directors,
   and animators..11%
▨ Architects..10%
■ Writers and authors..................................9%
■ Photographers..7%
■ Producers and directors............................7%

Source: National Endowment for the Arts, *Artists in the Workforce 1990–2005*, Washington, D.C., 2008.

Retailers certainly recognize the size and consumer preferences of techno-savvy Generation Y, colleges enjoy strong enrollments, and apartment owners profitably cater to these young adults and their mix-and-match roommates. However, their importance to Northern America's labor market and their potential real estate and consumer demands are not fully acknowledged. The older portion of this generation, who are currently renters, will become the first-time homebuyers who take advantage of bargain prices when the economy begins to recover. In massive numbers, they will furnish those houses, become Home Depot devotees, buy small cars, shop online, take "green" seriously, travel, go to concerts, and set new social and consumer trends of their own. For retailers, Generation Y is the hope for the future.

Some of the marked differences between the boomers and Generation Y are highlighted in figure 1-10. The highly mobile young people flock to urban areas, expect multiculturalism, and grasp globalization. They are already well traveled. Psychoanalyzing these two generations is fun, even though much of Generation Y is still in a formative stage. The somewhat arbitrary lists of remembered events at the bottom of figure 1-10 suggest a change in outlook: four of the items in the left column are international, if one classifies the attacks of September 11 that way. In contrast, Vietnam and putting a man on the moon are the only activities outside the United States in the right column.

The important takeaway is that a huge group of young people is preparing to reshape the U.S. economy. As the boomers did, they will change the workplace, entertainment, vacation travel, and residential communities.

GENERATION X Generation X is the smaller demographic group born from 1965 to 1976 that falls between the boomers and Generation Y. Although this cohort has not received the same attention, the transitional Generation X offer hints as to probable behavioral patterns of its successors.

One interesting characteristic is low fertility: 20 percent of women ages 40 to 44 are childless, twice the level of 30 years ago. Furthermore, the other 80 percent of the women have an average of 1.9 children versus 3.1 for their counterparts in 1976. Women with advanced academic degrees are more likely to be childless, suggesting that careers have often taken precedence over childrearing. Nevertheless, in 2006, 60 percent of all new mothers were working women. In Generation X, women married later and then bore their first child at a more advanced age as well. Early indications suggest a possible reversal of that pattern among Generation Y—perhaps because multitaskers believe they can successfully "do it all simultaneously"—but definitive data are not yet available.

CONTINUING IMMIGRATION Immigration fuels North American population growth, both upon arrival and later, as new residents have children in the United States and Canada. Thirty years ago, nearly two-thirds of all U.S. immigrants went to five states: California, New York, Texas, Florida, and Illinois. By 2005, the "big five's" share of arrivals was down to just over half and, with the exception of Maryland, the "second-tier" destinations (New Jersey, Massachusetts, Washington, and Virginia) also attracted fewer migrants than during the previous five years. Today's annual inflow of more than 1 million

Figure 1-10

Two Big U.S. Generations

	Generation Y	Baby Boomers
2007 size	73.9 million	75.6 million
2010 size	74.8 million	74.6 million
Born	1977 to 1994	1946 to 1964
Age now	15 to 32 years	45 to 63 years
Hispanic	19 percent	10 percent
African American	15 percent	12 percent
Asian	6 percent	5 percent
Foreign born	16 percent	14 percent
Dominant housing tenure	Renters	Owners
Neighborhood preference	Urban, walkable	Suburban, auto-oriented
Housing preferences	Affordable price, usable space	More space, more privacy
Mobility (moved in 2006 or 2007)	23.3 percent	7.5 percent
Expect never to retire	10 percent	25 percent
Live to work	16 percent	28 percent
Work to live	85 percent	72 percent
Communications	Cell phone, text messaging, Facebook, Twitter, blogs	Cell phone, e-mail
Generation-shaping events	Attacks of September 11, 2001 Fall of the Soviet Union Iraq war Challenger explosion Oklahoma City bombing Princess Diana's death Columbine iPods, video games YouTube, reality TV Hurricane Katrina	Civil rights movement The Beatles Vietnam Man on the moon Watergate Sexual revolution Roe v. Wade JFK, MLK, and RFK assassinations Woodstock Two-earner households

immigrants disperse throughout America, which means that residents of Tennessee, Iowa, and Georgia are being exposed to far more workers for whom English is a second language. Most native-born Americans are welcoming; but the combination of large numbers of immigrants, their movement to new destinations, and the fact that most are visually identifiable because they are Hispanic or Asian has also generated political backlash. As unemployment rises, some native-born workers will feel that immigrants pose an economic challenge as well.

The employment situation is complex. Sociologist Douglas S. Massey summarizes America's growing dependence on immigrant labor as follows:

> Competition in the increasingly globalized world economy has lowered the relative earnings of American industrial workers. As American consumers have benefited from cheaper, and often better, products and services from abroad, . . . the pressure to cut costs has encouraged many employers to look for employees willing to work harder for less compensation. . . . There is clearly a reciprocal dynamic between globalization, industrial restructuring, and immigration.
>
> Many individual American families, too, are purchasing more "immigrant labor" to replace traditional home-produced goods and services, including child care, lawn care, gardening, and food preparation (in restaurants, in grocery stores, or at home). The lower wages of immigrants have kept consumer prices lower in the United States than in other industrialized countries.[13]

This topic is covered more extensively in chapter 2, but several points are worth making here:

▸▸ Two key industries that have come to rely heavily on immigrant labor are construction and meat processing. According to sociologists Emilio Parrado and William Kandel, "As education levels in the general population rise and other employment options reduce the attractiveness of employment in these industries, American firms that do not or cannot locate production overseas seek cost-cutting measures at home."[14] Obviously, the construction trades cannot move offshore. They are not attracting enough native-born apprentices; as a consequence, 20 percent of all Mexican immigrants were working in construction at the peak of the boom.

▸▸ Partly because of the housing market collapse, the inflow of undocumented immigrants dropped from roughly 800,000 per year from 2000 to 2004 to an average of 500,000 annually between 2005 and 2008, with a considerably lower figure last year.[15]

▸▸ Nonetheless, the total number of undocumented residents in the United States grew from 8.4 million in 2000 to about 12 million today, or 4 percent of the American population. Four of five are Hispanic, with about 60 percent from Mexico.

▸▸ As unemployment rises, incomes of undocumented households fall. In 2008, remittances back to Mexico declined by 7 to 8 percent, and the flow of undocumented residents returning home increased.

Members of racial and ethnic minorities represent more than one-third of all Americans and are projected to represent a majority by 2050. Hispanic Americans now exceed 15 percent of the population and are growing faster than any other ethnic group. In fact, Hispanics account for half the country's population growth since 2000—60 percent from natural increase and 40 percent from immigration (a reversal of the ratios in the 1990s).

SLOWING MOBILITY In 2008, fewer than 12 percent of Americans changed residences, the lowest mobility since 1948. When boomers were children, back in the 1950s and 1960s, close to 20 percent of the population moved each year. Several factors explain today's moribund rate:

▸▸ Falling home prices and limited mortgage availability prevent homeowners from moving.

▸▸ In a recession, employed people hold onto their jobs and dismiss notions of moving and incurring the attendant expenses. Taking a new job seems risky when the last hired is often the first to be laid off.

▸▸ More two-career households in the labor force make geographic shifts complicated and therefore less frequent.

▸▸ Young people who cannot afford to live independently stay on with their parents—or move back.

▸▸ Since Proposition 13 passed, older Californians stay in their long-term homes to retain low property tax rates.

▸▸ Thanks to recent wealth reduction, fewer retirees are migrating to new locations.

As the economy recovers and as Generation Y becomes a larger force in homeowner-ship, mobility is likely to go back up—but only to 14 or 15 percent. Mobile people can move within the same metropolitan area, or they can switch to another city or state. A 2008 Pew Research Center survey[16] focused on the latter group and derived intriguing conclusions:

▸▸ Urbanites move more, rural dwellers less.

▸▸ Three-fourths of college graduates have moved away at least once from the metropolitan area where they grew up, versus half of those who have only high school diplomas.

▸▸ More affluent people are more likely to have moved to new locations one or more times.

▸▸ Half of all Midwestern adults report spending all their lives in their home metropolitan areas.

▸▸ The same is true of one-third of adults in the West; however, fewer than 14 percent of Nevada residents and only 28 percent of Arizonans were born in those states.

LATIN AMERICA AND THE CARIBBEAN

Over the past two to three years, institutional investors have focused on Latin American real estate, and an abundance of new funds have been raised, largely for development. The demographics support strong property demand going forward, with one caveat: the greatest need is for moderate- and middle-income—rather than luxury—product. Every country in Central and South America can use more shopping centers, workforce housing, inexpensive business hotels, logistics warehouses, and modern office space. Except for Puerto Rico, the economic focus in the Caribbean is heavily upon tourism, which is not going to flourish in the short term.

As shown in figure 1-11, all three subregions are growing steadily, though the Caribbean lags Central and South America. Central American nations will grow a bit faster, but the absolute number of additional people is two and a half times greater in South America. By 2030, South America will add more than 100 million residents, while the United States and Canada grow by less than 75 million.

Brazil, with 192 million people, and Mexico, with a population of 107 million, account for over half the total population in Latin America and the Caribbean. At 46 million,

Panama City: Central America's Dubai?

Of Panama's 3.5 million residents, 1 million live in Panama City, which has acquired an impressive skyline overlooking the Gulf of Panama and the ships awaiting passage or departing through the canal. Cranes are busy, with at least 5,000 high-rise apartment units and several hotels under construction. Although speculation in luxury units has a bubble aura, development continues. As a growing Latin American banking center, the second largest duty-free port after Hong Kong, and the operator and beneficiary of the canal, Panama's business activities are disproportional to the size of its population.

Long a popular expatriate community, with the countries of origin ebbing and flowing, Panama currently offers safe *pieds à terre* to Venezuelans, Ecuadoreans, Bolivians, and Colombians. As in Dubai, many condominiums are sold but unoccupied.

Panama City's downtown waterfront is one of the most polluted in the world, but a major cleanup is underway, with help from the Taiwanese. Part of the rehabilitation project is a new causeway that will relieve congestion on Balboa Boulevard.

Figure 1-12

Urbanization in Latin America and the Caribbean
2007 TO 2050

	PERCENTAGE URBANIZED		
	2007	2030	2050
Caribbean	65.4	75.5	82.6
Central America	70.8	77.7	83.3
South America	82.6	88.3	91.4
Selected Countries			
Argentina	91.8	94.6	96.0
Brazil	85.2	91.1	93.6
Chile	88.2	92.8	94.2
Costa Rica	62.8	73.8	81.5
Mexico	76.9	83.3	87.6
Panama	72.5	83.6	88.7
Peru	72.6	76.5	82.5
Total Region	**78.3**	**83.5**	**88.7**

Source: UN Population Division, *World Urbanization Prospects: The 2007 Revision*, tables A.1 and A.2. http://esa.un.org/unup.

Colombia is third, followed by Argentina's 40 million and then Peru and Venezuela, each with 28 million.

Latin America's economies focus on natural resource exports and, increasingly, on domestic consumer demand. Brazil is the world's largest exporter of coffee, beef, sugar, and orange juice and also ships massive quantities of soybeans, iron ore, and chickens. The country has formidable hydroelectric resources and now oil as well. Without destroying rainforest, Brazil has enough arable land to double its current agricultural usage.

Despite their emphasis on agriculture and natural resources, South American nations have urbanized rapidly over the last 30 years or so. As shown in figure 1-12, more than 78 percent of the Latin American and Caribbean population is urbanized; South America's proportion is 83 percent. Argentina's 92 percent and Chile's 88 percent stand out, as do the expected increases in urbanization in Panama and Costa Rica over the next 25 years. These kinds of increases have very positive economic effects. Fewer than 40 percent of Brazilians lived in cities 40 years ago; today, 85 percent are urbanites and the dynamism is palpable.

Sharp decreases in fertility accompanied rapid Latin American urbanization, as reflected in the recent data on average household sizes shown in figure 1-13. Not

Figure 1-11

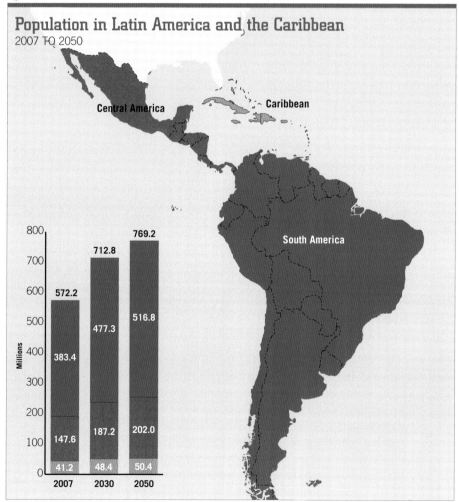

Source: UN Population Division, *World Urbanization Prospects: The 2007 Revision*, tables A.1 and A.5. http://esa.un.org/unup.

Figure 1-13

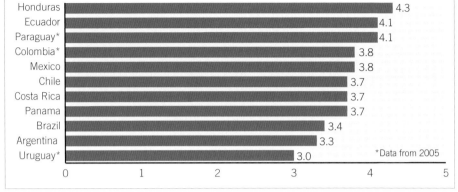

Average Household Size in Latin America
2006 (NUMBER OF PEOPLE)

Honduras	4.3
Ecuador	4.1
Paraguay*	4.1
Colombia*	3.8
Mexico	3.8
Chile	3.7
Costa Rica	3.7
Panama	3.7
Brazil	3.4
Argentina	3.3
Uruguay*	3.0

*Data from 2005

Source: Economic Commission for Latin America and the Caribbean, *Statistical Yearbook 2007*, table 1.1.13.

surprisingly, the three countries with more than four people per household are among the region's poorer nations.

Mexico's fertility rate decline is one of the most dramatic in the world—from 6.5 children per woman in 1970 to 2.2 today. (Over the same period, the world's fertility rate fell from 4.5 to 2.5.) Three factors contribute to Mexico's fertility pattern:

▸▸ Government-subsidized contraceptives and educational programs.

▸▸ Massive emigration of young men to the United States (an estimated 15 percent reduction in Mexico's male labor force between 1980 and 2000).

▸▸ Permanent migration of young people, both men and women, who subsequently had their children in the United States rather than in Mexico.

Mexico's negative migration rates are probably the largest of any developing country, though the Philippines intentionally sends a higher proportion of its workforce abroad. The United Nations suggests that Mexico could face a population decline by 2030, though there are indications of reverse migration between the United States and Mexico as jobs are eliminated in the former and economic opportunities present themselves in the latter.

Historically, Latin America has been faulted for income inequality—small percentages of wealthy families and tens of millions of peasants. Literacy improvements are modifying that profile and generating expanded numbers of moderate- and middle-income households throughout the region. Figure 1-14 summarizes the high literacy levels among young people in Latin America and the Caribbean: 96 percent overall, with a low of 88 percent for Caribbean nations and 97 percent in South America. The gender gap in education has essentially vanished in recent decades. Furthermore, secondary education is pervasive, even among poor young people.

Secondary school graduation and then university attendance create labor forces able to handle 21st-century jobs in the global economy; and Latin America is benefiting from a better educated young workforce, as evidenced by the rapid growth of employment within the formal economy. For instance, Peru's formal sector jobs are expanding at an annual rate of 9 percent. Once workers are able to document their pay, they can access credit—

Figure 1-14

Youth Literacy in Latin America and the Caribbean
(PERCENT)

	LITERATE 15- TO 24-YEAR-OLDS		
	Female	Male	Total
Caribbean	88.7	86.9	87.8
Central America	94.8	95.1	95.0
South America	97.9	96.7	97.3
Total Region	**96.4**	**95.6**	**96.0**

Source: United Nations, *World Youth Report 2007*, annex table 3.

for consumer durables, vehicles, and homes. In Mexico, mortgage payments are frequently deducted from borrowers' paychecks, so informal workers can be frozen out of the housing finance system.

The United Nations provides some perspective on the full-income picture: it estimates that 37 percent of Latin America's population is poor, and of those 195 million individuals, 71 million are indigent. Poverty rates are lowest in Chile, Uruguay, and Costa Rica. Thanks to spending on social programs in Brazil, the incomes of the bottom 10 percent of earners rose 58 percent from 2000 to 2006, while the incomes of the top 10 percent went up 7 percent. Even though 37 percent of Latin Americans are poor, 63 percent are not—and that is the important statistic for investors.

ASIA

As reflected in figure 1-15, both demographic and geographic size characterize Asia. Its 20 countries are extremely diverse—from landlocked Afghanistan, Nepal, and Mongolia to island nations like the Maldives, Indonesia, the Philippines, and Japan. With 57 percent of the earth's population, this continent will account for an even higher proportion of the global labor force for

Figure 1-15

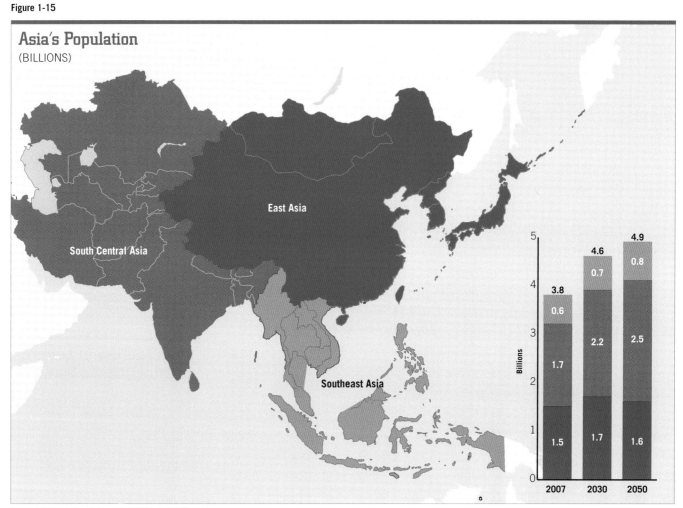

Source: UN Population Division, *World Urbanization Prospects: The 2007 Revision*, tables A.1 and A.5. http://esa.un.org/unup.

the foreseeable future; and it is rapidly creating moderate- and middle-class households that are avid spenders as well as savers. Simultaneously, Asia's differing cultures are growing increasingly interdependent—in trade, foreign investment, and tourism.

Because this is the least urbanized region after sub-Saharan Africa, it is where migration to towns and cities will be heaviest over the next 40 years, thereby generating unprecedented demand for infrastructure, houses, stores, warehouses, offices, and hotels. Looking at the lodging sector, Asian demand is broad and deep, though the greatest numerical need is for moderately priced facilities catering to domestic business and personal travelers. Over the next decade, Hilton Hotels Corporation wants to add 300 hotels to its current Asian inventory of roughly 50. Marriott International Inc. is doubling its accommodations; Accor S.A. has a big push on, especially with its three-star Ibis brand; and Starwood Hotels & Resorts Worldwide, Inc. has close to 100 new Asian hotels in its pipeline.

Figure 1-16 shows that, although less than 40 percent of Asia's population is urbanized today, the proportion will jump to 53 percent in 2030 and then to 65 percent by 2050. In numerical terms, the region's urban areas will add almost 950 million residents by 2030 and then another 750 million in the subsequent 20 years. Growth of this magnitude boggles the mind. As mentioned earlier, ten of the world's 19 megacities are in Asia; and by 2025, the region will have 15 of the world's 27. India and China will each have four, Japan and Pakistan will have two apiece, and Bangladesh, the Philippines, and Indonesia will each have one. Asia's ten largest countries are listed in figure 1-17. Between now and 2030, the only alterations in rank order will be that India and China will change places at the top, and the Philippines will move ahead of Japan in the middle.

Chapter 2 highlights the fact that Asia will provide the majority of this century's global workforce—at all skill levels. Although unskilled workers have lost assembly and construction jobs over the past year, serious shortages of skilled labor remain—in finance, medicine, research and development, law, engineering, software and computer services, accounting, pharmaceuticals, etc. As just one example, the emergence of low-cost airlines has triggered pilot poaching because the pool is inadequate. Managerial talent, especially to deal with multinational customers, is also in short supply. Many Asians who have been

Figure 1-16

Urbanization in Asia
2007 TO 2050

	PERCENTAGE URBANIZED		
	2007	2030	2050
Region Total	**39.4**	**52.9**	**65.2**
East Asia	46.1	62.4	71.4
South Central Asia	31.2	43.0	57.2
Southeast Asia	45.8	61.8	73.3
Selected Countries			
Bangladesh	26.6	36.2	51.5
China	42.2	62.4	74.1
India	29.2	40.6	55.2
Indonesia	50.4	68.9	79.4
Iran	68.0	77.9	84.1
Japan	66.3	73.0	80.1
Kazakhstan	36.1	66.8	75.9
Pakistan	35.7	49.8	63.7
Philippines	64.2	76.7	83.9
South Korea	81.2	86.3	89.8

Source: UN Population Division, *World Urbanization Prospects: The 2007 Revision*, tables A.1 and A.2. http://esa.un.org/unup.

Figure 1-17

Asia's Ten Largest Nations
2007 AND 2030 (MILLIONS)

Country	2007 Population	Rank	Country	2030 Population
China	1,329	1	India	1,506
India	1,169	2	China	1,458
Indonesia	232	3	Indonesia	280
Pakistan	164	4	Pakistan	240
Bangladesh	159	5	Bangladesh	218
Japan	128	6	Philippines	122
Philippines	88	7	Japan	118
Vietnam	87	8	Vietnam	110
Iran	71	9	Iran	91
Thailand	64	10	Thailand	69

Note: Population of China does not include Hong Kong and Macau.

Source: UN Population Division, *World Urbanization Prospects: The 2007 Revision.*

living in Europe and Northern America are returning to their homelands to fill these gaps, capitalizing on their language fluency and understanding of Western cultures. As skills shortages develop, competitors attempt to recruit each other's trained employees, and that in turn leads to wage escalation and high turnover. At some managerial levels, pay in India and China can be comparable to that in Europe or the United States—but the wages buy a far more pampered lifestyle.

Demography is creating labor problems as well—in Japan, South Korea, and China, where workforces will shrink between now and 2050. Like Europe, which is analyzed in chapter 5, East Asia faces negative population growth, as outlined below.

JAPAN Along with Russia, Japan offers a prototype of demographic decline. Japan's birthrate dropped below the replacement level of 2.1 children per woman back in the 1970s and by 2006, it was 1.36. Even though life expectancy has increased steadily—from just over 50 years in 1949 to the current 82 years—the country's population actually began to decline in 2005. From today's total of 128 million residents, the National Institute of Population and Social Security Research expects Japan's population to fall to 95 million by 2050. Even though the average annual decrease of 767,000 people will be lower than Russia's loss of 1 million, it will prompt major economic adjustment. The number of households is still rising in Japan; but in 2007, one-person households became the dominant category.

From a real estate standpoint, Japan will experience an absolute reduction in demand and an excess of supply. Rural villages are literally disappearing, and many municipalities will need to shrink. Perhaps fortuitously, Japanese housing has never been intended to outlast the household that builds it. As summarized in *The Economist*, "Where 89 percent of British homes have had more than one owner, and 78 percent of homes in America and 66 percent in France, only 13 percent of Japanese homes have ever been resold."[17] Because value is perceived to be in the land, not the building, homes are typically demolished after 30 years or so. Clearly, replacement demand will exist for all types of real estate, but there will have to be a net reduction in space as Japan's population shrinks by the equivalent of Malaysia plus Hong Kong.

Two demographic patterns that pose enormous challenges for Japan (and East Asia generally) are a rising senior population and a declining labor force. Just after World War II, only 5 percent of Japan's residents were over age 65; today, the figure is 20 percent and it will reach 25 percent by 2015. Retirement generally occurs at 60, so Japan's companies are losing a formidable talent pool. At the other end of the worker age spectrum, 16 million Japanese are currently in their twenties, but the number will drop by 3 million over the next decade. Today's workforce of 66.5 million could decline by more than one-third between now and 2050.

SOUTH KOREA If Japan is the high-income shrinking country in Eastern Asia, the middle-income one is South Korea, where average per capita income of $20,000 is half that of Japan. With a total population of 48 million—and falling—South Korea is 38 percent the size of its affluent neighbor to the east. In a region of declining birthrates, South Korea's has fallen the most sharply, from 4.5 children per woman in 1970 to 1.26 in 2008. Again, the population is aging and the workforce is contracting. South Korea's national pension scheme and long-term care plan for the elderly are only about 20 years old, so funding is not adequate for the higher dependency ratios ahead.

CHINA South Korea's situation is writ large in China. Despite being the world's most populous country, with more than 1.3 billion residents, China's one-child policy has held the population down by 400 million since 1979, according to the National Population and Family Planning Commission. Today's fertility rate of 1.4 or 1.5 is slightly above Japan's and South Korea's but far below replacement level. The results of the past 30 years' demographic policies are a high and rising proportion of seniors, a workforce that will begin to shrink in 2015, and a disproportionate number of males to females.

Melbourne's Downtown Demographics

Over the past 20 years, the city center of Melbourne, Australia, has been revitalized, thanks to a visionary goal of transforming the central business district into a central activities district for a metropolitan area of 4 million residents. Among the changes:

➤ Birrarung Marr, a new 20.5-acre park along the Yarra River with canals, paths, bridges, and event venues.

➤ Federation Square, built over an operating railyard to connect the city center with the Yarra River. It's the new heart of downtown.

➤ Renovation of City Square, a 30,000-square-foot public space offering a range of seating and activity centers.

➤ Postcode 3000, a city program that added 3,000 residential units in central Melbourne.

➤ An explosion of outdoor cafes, from two in 1983 to 356 in 2004.

➤ Transformation of alleys into traffic-free "little streets" with restaurants, microretailers, and seating areas.

➤ Public art installations, both permanent and temporary.

➤ Increased college and university enrollments.

➤ Burgeoning pedestrian traffic.

➤ Employment growth.

Source: Sam Newberg, "Melbourne Reborn," *Urban Land*, October 2008, pp. 109–15.

China has no Medicare or Social Security equivalent, and other social safety nets are minimal. Consequently, Chinese households save at prodigious rates, with urbanites reserving one-quarter of their incomes; that share is actually going up. However, the situation is tougher for Chinese people who were working adults during the Cultural Revolution: fewer than half of older urban citizens have any savings, and elderly farmers are in even more dire straits.

An estimated 130 million Chinese workers from rural villages—both men and women—migrate to factory, construction, and other unskilled or semiskilled jobs throughout the country. This "floating population" is not counted among urban residents because their home bases are the villages where their children and parents remain. Migrant workers remit part of their earnings back home, to cover school fees, clothing purchases, televisions, etc. With the cutback in exports last year, a government survey suggested that at least 25 million such migrants will be looking for new work—because 20 million lost their jobs and the pool normally grows by 6 or 7 million people annually. It is hard to know how many of the job losses resulted from normal seasonal turnover that occurs around Chinese New Year versus permanent job loss; however, the government is paying close attention and is anxious to avoid uprisings by unemployed villagers.

Independent of these migrant workers, China's urban population expanded from 254 million to 601 million from 1990 to 2007, with more people reclassified through the extension of urban boundaries than by actual migration. Between now and 2025, China's urban areas are expected to add the equivalent of the total U.S. population, and two-thirds of those newcomers will be migrants from rural areas. By 2025, China's 926 million urbanites will reside in 219 cities of more than 1 million people. Of those, 24 will house more than 5 million; and as discussed earlier, at least four megacities will have over 10 million. Because of China's centralized government, policies can be changed swiftly, so predictions are less certain than elsewhere. Nonetheless, new and expanding urban markets will generate almost incomprehensibly large and diverse investment opportunities.

Medium-sized cities with 1.5 to 5 million people will attract 40 percent of growth, produce the greatest housing demand, and see the biggest increases in their middle classes. Just think of all the new retail stores. The McKinsey Global Institute says, "The change wrought by urbanization on this scale will be spectacular. . . . During this period [to 2025, China] will . . . erect 20,000 to 50,000 skyscrapers (for about 40 billion square meters of new floor space)."[18]

OCEANIA

By far the smallest of the world's geographic regions, Oceania's 2007 population was only 34.3 million, or 0.5 percent of global residents. Australia and New Zealand, as shown in figure 1-18, dominate the region, accounting for 73 percent of the population. As migration to that subregion continues, Oceania is expected to experience 26 percent growth between now and 2030, the second highest rate after Africa and the Middle East. Oceania's other nations are small islands, with Fiji in Melanesia being the only one coming close to having a million inhabitants. In the aggregate, Papua New Guinea contains 6.3 million people.

Melanesia is distinct in having the lowest urbanization rate among the world's sub-regions—only 18.7 percent, as highlighted in figure 1-19. The rate will nearly double by 2050, but only to 35.8 percent; no other subregion will be less than half urbanized at mid-century. Fiji and New Caledonia are more than 50 percent urban now, but Papua New Guinea's proportion is only 12.5 percent.

In contrast, at 88.2 percent, Australia and New Zealand is the most urbanized subregion in the world. By 2050, 93.5 percent of its people will live in cities or suburbs. Both countries grow steadily, thanks to immigration: between 20 and 25 percent of this subregion's residents were born elsewhere.

Tourism is a mainstay of many Oceania locations, whether it is diving off Palau or along the Great Barrier Reef, fishing in New Zealand's glacial lakes, high-end shopping in Guam targeted to Japanese visitors, relaxing at beach resorts, or attending the opera in Sydney. Though Japanese tourism has declined somewhat, Taiwanese and South Koreans are picking up the slack. For Europeans and Americans, Oceania is remote enough that travel requires a serious commitment of time and money.

Figure 1-19

Urbanization in Oceania
2007 TO 2050

	PERCENTAGE URBANIZED		
	2007	2030	2050
Australia and New Zealand	88.2	91.5	93.5
Melanesia	18.7	24.7	35.8
Micronesia	67.3	73.1	79.9
Polynesia	42.4	52.2	63.8
Region Total	**70.5**	**72.6**	**76.4**

Source: UN Population Division, *World Urbanization Prospects: The 2007 Revision*, tables A.1 and A.2. http://esa.un.org/unup.

Figure 1-18

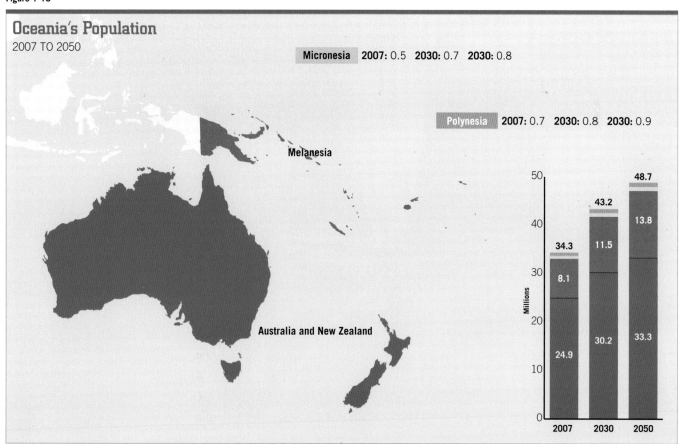

Oceania's Population
2007 TO 2050

Micronesia   2007: 0.5   2030: 0.7   2030: 0.8

Polynesia   2007: 0.7   2030: 0.8   2030: 0.9

Melanesia

Australia and New Zealand

Labor | 2

In absolute terms, the globe's labor force will expand dramatically between now and 2030. The number of working-age men and women (between ages 15 and 64) will rise almost 30 percent—from 4.2 billion in 2005 to 5.4 billion in 2030. Half the increase will occur in Asia, as reflected in figure 2-1, and nearly two-thirds of the remainder will be in sub-Saharan Africa. The Anglo-American nations of Canada, the United States, Ireland, the United Kingdom, Australia, and New Zealand will experience labor force growth, but at far lower levels than over the past four decades.

As discussed in chapter 5, continental Europe faces sobering challenges because it will be the only region with workforce shrinkage—a loss of 11 percent between now and 2030. Asia's strong overall growth masks the downward trends in a few countries: significant labor force contraction issues are arising in Japan, South Korea, and China.

In the short and medium terms, the challenge will be to create meaningful work for all the young people entering the global workforce. If the challenge is met to a reasonable extent, the potential for economic growth in one emerging market after another will be exciting. If young people graduate from high school and college and then cannot find work, as is common in Greece and much of Africa today, unrest and instability will abound. Needless to say, the global recession puts a damper on job creation and frightens families in emerging markets, who were just becoming comfortable with discretionary spending and were making aggressive plans for their futures. Their newfound caution will color future behavior.

Globally, the percentage of 15- to 64-year-olds in the total population will increase only slightly by 2030, as reflected in figure 2-2. Sharp drops will occur in the developed

Figure 2-1

Regional Working-Age Population
2005 AND 2030 (MILLIONS)

	2005	2030	CHANGE Number	CHANGE Percent
Sub-Saharan Africa	411.6	784.2	372.7	90.6
MENA	229.5	349.2	119.7	52.2
Latin America and the Caribbean	356.5	472.5	116.0	32.5
Asia	2,451.3	3,098.3	647.0	26.4
Oceania	21.7	27.1	5.5	25.2
Northern America	223.1	252.6	29.5	13.2
Europe	498.8	446.0	-52.8	-10.6
World	**4,192.4**	**5,430.0**	**1,237.6**	**29.5**

Source: UN Population Division, *World Population Prospects: The 2006 Revision*, http://esa.un.org/unpp.

Figure 2-2

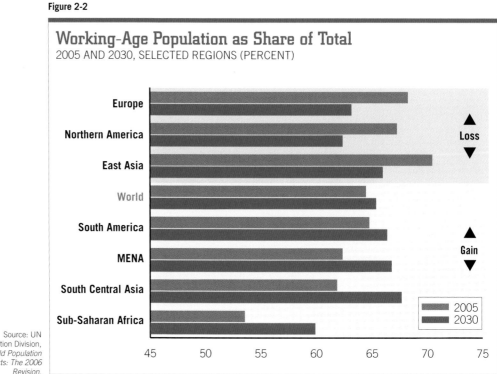

Working-Age Population as Share of Total
2005 AND 2030, SELECTED REGIONS (PERCENT)

Source: UN
Population Division,
*World Population
Prospects: The 2006
Revision.*

world, which means rising dependency ratios—the number of children and retirees rely-ing on each worker's productivity. In contrast, regions at the bottom of figure 2-2 will experience "demographic dividends"[1]—the working-age share of their population will grow and can generate strong economic gains. The developed world enjoyed such divi-dends from the post–World War II baby boom generation; it now faces the social service and pension costs of an aging populace. Looking ahead, the demographic dividend favors developing regions where fertility rates have dropped recently—South Central Asia (including Bangladesh, India, Iran, and Pakistan) and Central America, which is not shown in the figure but has a similar profile. South American nations fall between the developed and developing world: their fertility rates have declined sharply but they also have large aging populations.

Lower fertility is highly correlated with economic growth in emerging markets, partly because school attendance is higher in families with fewer children. The virtuous cycle is that the better educated get higher-paying jobs and send their children for even more educa-tion so they can obtain even more challenging employment. And onward and upward. In poor countries overwhelmed by children, it is hard to kick-start this cycle.

Figure 2-2 also illustrates why there is no retreat from offshoring, which is used to take advantage of the global workforce. Lenovo, now the world's third largest computer maker, is structured around hubs of expertise: hardware design in Japan, marketing in India, and manufacturing in China. The chief executive officer calls it "worldsourcing." For years, garment producers have migrated from one country to another to take advan-tage of low-cost labor. Now, a broad range of manufacturers and servicers are using the same strategy.

Figure 2-3a

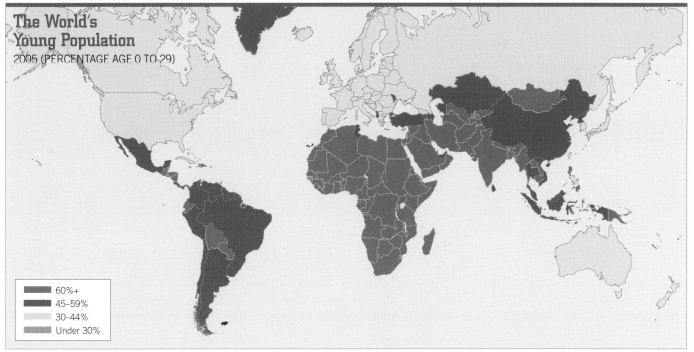

The World's
Young Population
2005 (PERCENTAGE AGE 0 TO 29)

- 60%+
- 45–59%
- 30–44%
- Under 30%

Figure 2-3b

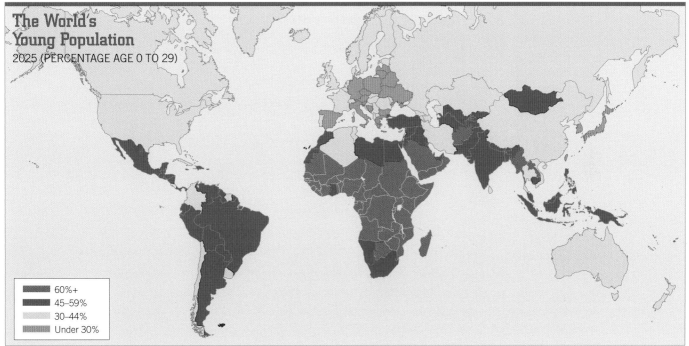

The World's
Young Population
2025 (PERCENTAGE AGE 0 TO 29)

- 60%+
- 45–59%
- 30–44%
- Under 30%

Global aging—the single most influential demographic trend for the first half of this century—dictates that labor force maturation will also be a critical issue. Furthermore, declining overall fertility rates mean that fewer young people will enter many nations' work forces. Figure 2-3 shows where the concentrations of people under age 30 are greatest and lowest in 2005 and 2025. Because fertility rates remain high in sub-Saharan Africa and the Arabian Peninsula, large proportions of new labor force entrants will be concentrated there. The global challenge is that in 2030 most of the very young countries will also be poor; they lack the robust education systems that will teach young people to read and write, let alone provide them with marketable skills.

Labor Force Participation

Not all working-age people choose to work, and of those choosing employment, not all can find it. At the younger end of the 15-to-64 age spectrum are students still attending high school, college, and graduate school; the older end encompasses early retirees. So the people actually working or looking for jobs (the labor force) are far fewer than the total working-age population. Among the many reasons for not working are lack of skills, lack of accessible transportation to a job, disability or poor health, full-time care of family members, and cultural restrictions (particularly for women).

Roughly 3 billion people were employed around the world last year, an increase of 1.3 percent over 2007, which was well below the average growth rate of 1.6 percent of the past ten years.[2] Just over 60 percent of the age-eligible population is working now: three-fourths of all men and half of the women. Because of rising school attendance, workforce participation among young people had been dropping for a long time, though it leveled off over the past three years. Youth unemployment reached 76 million in 2008, whereas 114 million adults were looking for work[3]; obviously, unemployment is skewed toward young people.

Three subregions experienced increases in employment-to-population ratios between 1998 and 2008: Latin America and the Caribbean with the largest change, the Middle East and North Africa (MENA), and Central and Southeast Europe. Greater participation by women boosted the figures in all these regions. In sub-Saharan Africa, the ratio was nearly unchanged.

Employment and Income

The high employment-to-population ratios seen in sub-Saharan Africa and South Asia in no way ensure that working people in poor countries are able to support their families. Work is loosely defined by the United Nations' International Labour Office (ILO) and the Bureau of Labor Statistics in the United States. It can consist of only a few hours of employment per day or per week, either as a paid employee or as an unpaid worker in a family business. Work includes subsistence farming, peddling goods, or providing household domestic services.

Important strides have been made in reducing global poverty levels, but millions of people who work are still very poor. Using recently updated poverty standards and measurement methods developed by the World Bank and others, the ILO estimates that 609 million working people earned less than $1.25 a day in 2007. The good news is that the number of extremely poor workers declined by more than 25 percent over the previous ten years; the bad news is that one in five workers still has meager earnings. And as discussed in chapter 3, because of rising prices for basic needs, economists now see $2 a day as a more realistic measure of poverty. By that standard, 40 percent of global workers were

Figure 2-4

The Working Poor by Income per Day
1997 AND 2007 (PERCENT OF TOTAL EMPLOYMENT)

	EARNING <$1.25 A DAY		EARNING <$2 A DAY	
	1997	2007	1997	2007
Central and Southeast Europe	8.2	5.1	21.5	13.9
Latin America and the Caribbean	12.9	6.8	27.8	16.4
Middle East	9.7	9.0	25.8	24.0
Northern Africa	11.8	9.8	42.0	30.2
East Asia	38.4	10.4	69.2	33.0
World	**32.7**	**20.6**	**54.2**	**40.6**
Southeast Asia and the Pacific	35.6	16.4	63.2	46.6
South Asia	57.2	47.1	86.3	80.9
Sub-Saharan Africa	65.0	58.3	85.4	82.2

Source: ILO, Trends Econometric Models, December 2008.

poor in 2007. In South Asia and sub-Saharan Africa, the working poor exceed 80 percent of total employment, as shown in figure 2-4.

In addition to the poor, the ILO cites "vulnerable" workers—those who work without pay (usually for family members) in return for food and shelter, those who maintain subsistence farms, and those who do not earn a salary. Their share of total employment in 2007 is estimated at a staggering 51 percent, with modest improvement seen since 1997. These workers are generally unable to take advantage of such government-funded social "safety net" programs as exist, so they are especially at risk during economic downturns.

Working Women

With female employment at 49 percent of all women on a global basis, compared with 73 percent of men, women provide a large, underutilized labor supply. Women's participation grew strongly in the 1980s and 1990s, but that trend began to reverse over the past ten years, partly because young women are staying in school longer—thereby becoming qualified for better jobs. The largest gaps in male and female participation in employment are in MENA and South Asia (India, Pakistan, Bangladesh, Iran). East Asia has the smallest gap, largely because of relative gender equality within China's massive labor force.

A few other generalizations about working women:

▸ They are more inclined than men to be wage or salary workers.

▸ They constitute the bulk of "contributing family workers," whether on small farms, in retail shops, doing simple assembly of goods, or creating marketable handiwork.

▸ Women are less likely to be employers than employees.

▸ Expansion of part-time job opportunities pulls women into the labor force.

▸ As economies shift toward services, more positions open up for women.

▸ The greater a woman's education, the more likely she is to work and the higher her wages will be.[4]

▸ Educated women are better farmers, achieving higher yields.[5]

Figure 2-5 shows labor force participation rates for ten developed countries in 2007—for both sexes together and for women alone. With the exceptions of Italy and Japan, at least 51 percent of women were participating. Canada's 63 percent is the highest rate and ahead of Sweden, which is often cited for its women- and family-friendly social support systems.

Participation rates have risen since 1960 in just half the nations shown in figure 2-5—the United States, Canada, Australia, the Netherlands, and the United Kingdom—and the gains are all attributable to more working women. Male participation declined across the board. For example, in 1960 the rates in the United States were 83 percent for men and 38 percent for women, and now the comparable figures are 73 and 59 percent.

Italy stands out as a place where far fewer people work—both men and women. Italians are accustomed to retiring in their early fifties and, with a rapidly aging worker profile, retirements have seriously eroded the size of the labor force. Japan had the most pronounced drop in total labor force participation over the past 50 years—from about 68 percent in 1960 down to 60 percent in 2007.

Economic Sector Shifts

Global economic change is clearly reflected in figure 2-6. As nations evolve along the development spectrum and workers move from rural to urban areas to take new jobs, employment transitions from subsistence farming to manufacturing and services. Agriculture does not disappear but farms become larger, use more productive seeds and fertilizers, switch to mechanical tools, and require less labor.

Worldwide, service employment represents more than 43 percent of the total, has moved well ahead of agriculture (34 percent), and continues to rise steadily. Industrial jobs constitute the remaining 23 percent of employment, a proportion that has remained fairly steady over the last dozen years. However, regional employment profiles can vary dramatically from global norms. As indicated in figure 2-6, much of the developing world's population is still rural and operating subsistence farms. In sub-Saharan Africa, 62 percent of workers are in agriculture, many of them women maintaining family farms while men take

Figure 2-5

Source: U.S. Bureau of Labor Statistics.

*2006 data

Figure 2-6

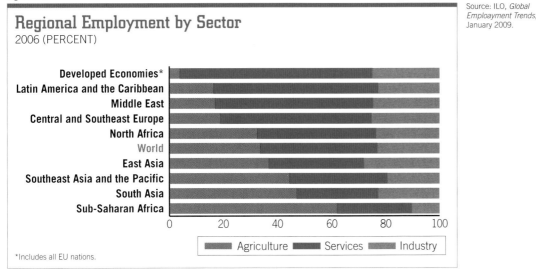

Regional Employment by Sector
2006 (PERCENT)

Source: ILO, *Global Emploayment Trends*, January 2009.

*Includes all EU nations.

jobs elsewhere. About 45 percent of all jobs in Southeast Asia, the Pacific island nations, and South Asia are still agricultural.

Contrast this with developed nations, where only 4 percent of all jobs are still in agriculture, 25 percent are in industry, and services account for more than 70 percent of jobs. Latin America, where urbanization began to accelerate 30 or 40 years ago, is the developing region with the highest proportion of service employment and the smallest share in agriculture. The Middle East is the next lowest in agriculture (much of its land is arid and not tillable), followed by Central and Southeast Europe, which includes the former Soviet republics. As would be expected with China's and South Korea's focus on manufacturing growth, East Asia has the highest proportion of jobs in the industrial sector. Where service employment dominates, people can more easily work until later in life because they are less likely to wear out physically or be injured on the job. Also, women can move in and out of service jobs to accommodate child rearing.

Labor Productivity

According to the ILO, worker productivity rose worldwide by about 25 percent between 1996 and 2006. As shown in figure 2-7, the greatest change was in East Asia, where output per worker doubled. Second was Central and Southeast Europe with a 54 percent increase. South Asia ranked third with productivity growth of 48 percent over the ten-year period. In contrast, the Middle East had essentially no change in productivity.

In absolute terms, productivity in the developed world was estimated at $62,952 per employed person in 2006. The Middle East was the developing region with the highest productivity, at $21,910 per worker on a purchasing power parity basis, thanks largely to oil revenues. Latin America and the Caribbean, at $18,908 per employed person, was next highest, followed by Central and Southeast Europe. Despite steady growth in emerging markets, the average developed country worker produced five times more value than an East Asian worker and more than 12 times the output of a typical sub-Saharan African worker.

"A 2005 London Business School study . . . concluded that for every additional 10 mobile phones per 100 people, a country's GDP rises 0.5 percent."

—Sara Corbett, "Can the Cellphone Help End Global Poverty?", p. 38

Source: ILO, Global
Employment Trends Model.

Figure 2-7

Change in Labor Productivity, 1996 to 2006
VALUE ADDED PER EMPLOYED PERSON (CONSTANT 2000 US$ AT PPP)

	1996	2006	Change (Percent)
Developed Economies*	52,876	62,952	19.1
Middle East	22,130	21,910	-1.0
World	**15,824**	**19,834**	**25.3**
Latin America and the Caribbean	17,652	18,908	7.1
Central and Southeast Europe	11,787	18,121	53.7
North Africa	12,967	14,751	13.8
East Asia	6,347	12,591	98.4
Southeast Asia and the Pacific	8,068	9,419	16.7
South Asia	5,418	7,998	47.6
Sub-Saharan Africa	4,490	5,062	12.7

*Includes all EU nations.

"A global study by Expedia.com found that about a third of employed Americans usually do not take all the vacation days that they are entitled to, leaving an average of three days on the table. This is not so unusual. About a quarter of the workers in Britain do not take all their vacation time, and in France a little less. The only difference is that the British get an average of 26 days of vacation and the French about 37—compared with our 14 days."

—Alina Tugend, "Vacations Are Good for You, Medically Speaking," *The New York Times*, June 7, 2008

To a large extent, the differences in productivity tie to the type of work being done, as well as the way it is performed. For example, productivity is far higher in an almost totally automated facility that manufactures expensive goods than in manual assembly of low-cost items. Developed countries specialize in the former and China, Vietnam, and other developing countries in the latter. The United States, at $63,885 per worker in 2006, exhibited the greatest productivity, with Ireland second at $55,986 and then Luxembourg at $55,641. Both Ireland and Luxembourg have small workforces.

In terms of annual time worked per person, six Asian nations exceeded 2,200 hours in 2006: Bangladesh, China, Malaysia, South Korea, Sri Lanka, and Thailand. In contrast, workers in most European countries put in far fewer hours: less than 1,600 per year in Belgium, Denmark, France, Germany, the Netherlands, and Sweden.

Education

A key contributor to more productive labor forces is education, which is progressively improving. In most nations, illiteracy rates are lower for youth than for adults, so the average child is developing a stronger skill base than his or her parents. Even so, the bulk of the global labor supply still consists of workers with low or medium skill sets. Consequently, globally strong demand, combined with an inadequate supply of workers with tertiary-level education and superior skills, is pushing wages up for highly skilled labor and widening the pay gaps among skill levels.

The recent report by the United Nations Education, Scientific, and Cultural Organization (UNESCO), *Overcoming Inequality: Why Governance Matters*, describes a "vast gulf" in educational opportunity between rich and poor countries:

▸▸ One in three children in developing countries (193 million in total) reaches primary school age having had their brain development and education prospects impaired by malnutrition—a figure that rises to four in ten children in parts of South Asia. In some countries, high economic growth has done little to reduce child malnutrition.

▸▸ Some 75 million children of primary school age are not in school, including just under one-third of the relevant age group in sub-Saharan Africa.

▶ Child labor is also a barrier to education; an estimated 214 million children were working in 2004, of which 166 million were between ages 5 and 14.

▶ School attendance among slum-dwelling children can be 20 percentage points lower than for other urban children. In some countries, children living in slums show attendance rates lower than those of children in rural areas.

▶ Over a third of children in rich countries complete a university degree, whereas in much of sub-Saharan Africa, a smaller share completes only primary education—and just 5 percent receive university-level schooling.

▶ Millions of children who start school drop out before completing primary school.[6]

Retirement

In more affluent, developed economies, workers have become accustomed to earlier and earlier retirement—in one's fifties if possible:

▶ Americans can tap into Social Security at 62, albeit with lower payments than they would receive at age 66 or 67.

▶ In Taiwan, the average retirement age hit an all-time low of under 55 in 2004.

▶ The typical Korean worker leaves corporate employment at 54 but then works part-time or in low-wage jobs for another 14 years before finally retiring at 68.

▶ In Europe, the highest statutory pensionable age is 67, for workers in Norway and Iceland.

▶ Japan raised its pension age to 65; it had been 57 for women and 60 for men.

"Besides the gains in primary enrollment, the most impressive development in educational attainment in Asia has been the dramatic upsurge in enrollment at the tertiary level. Globally, the number of students in tertiary education doubled between 1990 and 2004, reaching 132 million. East Asia and the Pacific led the trend with an increase of 25 million students during this period. In China alone, the number of students in tertiary education doubled between 1998 and 2002 and again between 2001 and 2004. By 2004, China had 19 million tertiary students, the largest number of any country and 15 percent of the world total. . . . The substantial increase in Asian tertiary enrollment is largely a response to demographic exigencies, as countries have had to invest heavily in the education sector to meet the growing demand for schooling among members of the youth bulge."

—United Nations, *World Youth Report 2007*, pp. 11–12

▸▸ In Italy, fewer than a third of 55- to 64-year-olds are working or looking for employment, and labor force participation by people 65 and older is only 3 percent. The situation in Austria is comparable.

▸▸ French workers typically retire at 60.

▸▸ In contrast, the highest participation among 55- to 64-year-olds is in Sweden (73 percent), followed by Norway at 69 percent and Japan at 67 percent—all more than twice as committed to work as Italians and Austrians.

▸▸ When it comes to working past 65, Mexico stands out with 29 percent of the labor force participating. Japan and Portugal are at 20 percent and 18 percent, respectively.

Today's older people are far healthier and have longer life expectancies than their predecessors—to the point that some say 60 is the new 40. Yet retirement ages have fallen. In developed nations that focus on services, fewer workers are physically challenged in their jobs and could easily work past traditional retirement age. Over the next 20 years, Japan's working-age population will decline by 15 percent while its 65-and-older population expands by 50 percent. That decline could be ameliorated if more seniors remained in the labor force. Europe's prospects are better than Japan's but worse than America's. As described in chapter 5, European countries are facing high dependency ratios, but their electorates vote down retirement benefit modifications, and immigration is a touchy subject.

As portrayed in figure 2-8, the proportion of the United States labor force that is age 55 or older will increase from 16 percent in 2005 to 23 percent by 2030. Last year, the oldest baby boomers turned 62 and became eligible to collect Social Security benefits. By 2011, the same people will begin to use Medicare. Since 1995, labor force participation rates have risen for both men and women over 55. Opinion polls consistently report that boomers intend to work longer, with as many as one-quarter claiming they will never retire. Among the factors contributing to an increase in older workers: legislation that eliminates mandated retirement, better overall health, inadequate retirement savings, and erosion of 401(k) assets.

Several observations can be made about retirement prospects in developed nations:

▸▸ Raising labor force participation among older workers is verging on mandatory, in order to keep government pension schemes solvent.

▸▸ Today's economic environment will force many people to keep working longer. A recent AARP survey of American baby boomers found 34 percent saying they were thinking of delaying retirement. *The McKinsey Quarterly* says, "The low savings rate and extensive liabilities of the boomer have left about two-thirds of them unprepared for retirement."[7] That was before the latest stock market and home price declines. Many people will have no choice about continuing to work.

▸▸ One way to compensate for higher dependency ratios is to increase the productivity of the remaining workers with technology, reengineered work processes, and offshoring of low-value operations to countries with younger labor forces. By extending the working time of potential retirees, nations can gain time to streamline their economic activities.

▸▸ As a result of retirements, shortages are emerging in skilled trades and professions—from plumbers and electricians to nuclear engineers. Young people need to be trained as replacements for retirees with vital skills.

▸▸ More guest worker programs may be introduced.

Labor Migration

Both urbanization (migration within nations) and labor movement among countries were themes of *Global Demographics 2008*. New data are available on both topics. External migration and remittances sent back to countries of origin are covered here, whereas urbanization is featured in chapters 1, 5, and 6.

About 200 million people live outside their country of origin, with half of them having moved from one developing country to another. Labor migration has accelerated in this century, though the global recession will alter migration patterns. On the one hand, the push to go abroad is even stronger from poor home countries; but on the other hand, unemployment is rising in recipient countries, so jobs are harder to find, especially for unskilled laborers. Also, as unemployment rises, backlashes occur in receiving countries (as in Russia, South Africa, Italy, and the United States).

Figure 2-8

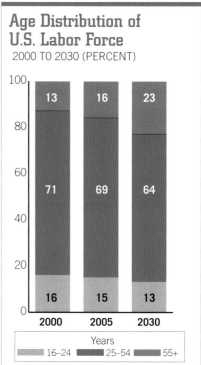

Age Distribution of U.S. Labor Force
2000 TO 2030 (PERCENT)

Source: U.S. Bureau of Labor Statistics.

The reasons for labor migration are straightforward: receiving nations have work to be done, and the pay is appealing to incoming migrants who typically benefit from a fivefold salary increase when going from a poor location to a rich one. Inadequate opportunities at home push most migrant workers abroad. A few observations on growing labor mobility and its effects:

▸ In the Philippines, sending labor elsewhere has been an explicit economic development strategy for years—to the point that nearly 10 percent of the total labor force works outside the country. About 30 percent are in the United States, but it is said that Filipinos are working in every nation except North Korea.

▸ For smaller countries, remittances can represent a substantial share of GDP (for example, 46 percent in Tajikistan, 38 percent in Moldova, and 24 percent in Lebanon in 2007). In addition, people going abroad reduce the competition for jobs among remaining workers.

▸ Developed countries need highly skilled workers in mathematics, engineering, information technology, medicine, and the like. The longer-term solution is to produce such people through the education system, but the short-term answer is to import them. The six Anglo-American[8] countries and many nations of continental Europe have explicit programs to attract skilled workers.

▸ Loss of highly skilled citizens would appear to create a brain drain in the emerging world, but a portion of their higher offshore pay generally filters back home. According to the World Bank, "Cross-country research on the determinants of economic growth has not found evidence of a negative impact associated with the emigration of people with skills."[9] Moreover, reverse migration is becoming more common, with earlier migrants or their children returning to their countries of origin to take advantage of today's job opportunities. Even though salaries may be lower, purchasing power is far greater and the culture is comfortable. This way, what might originally have seemed like a brain drain becomes "brain circulation."

▸ The proportion of highly skilled emigrants from all developing regions has risen sharply over the past 15 years, while the share of low-skilled outmigrants has dropped even more dramatically. The latter may have more opportunities at home as their nations' economies improve. Also, the legal barriers to migration for those without employer sponsorship have become both difficult and expensive to navigate.

▸ Political and religious refugees constitute a share of migrants, albeit a small one.

Figure 2-9

Top Migration Targets
BY REASON

Rank	Attractiveness to Migrants	Accessibility to Migrants	Need for Migrants
1	United States	Australia	Japan
2	United Kingdom	Canada	Italy
3	Australia	Singapore	Portugal
4	Norway	New Zealand	Finland
5	France	Israel	Czech Republic

Sources: Economist Intelligence Unit and Western Union, 2008.

More and more business executives take global assignments. They tend to be flexible people who are interested in other cultures, have language skills, handle change well, and tolerate uncertainty. Most global firms try to develop local managers to handle the business in their own countries, so international assignments may simply be transitional.

For large construction projects—infrastructure and commercial real estate—project managers are often drawn from the pool of itinerant global experts.

More than half the world's migrant workers are now women, many employed in health care and services.

A 2008 study commissioned by Western Union evaluates 61 countries on three criteria: their need to attract immigrants to maintain economic growth, their socioeconomic appeal to inmigrants, and their legal accessibility. As shown in figure 2-9, the five countries most in need of immigrants—Japan, Italy, Portugal, Finland, and the Czech Republic—do not appear among the leaders in either appeal or accessibility. France is a slight exception because it is seventh on the list of countries most in need of immigrants and fifth in overall attractiveness. (Of the countries needing newcomers, nine of the top ten are in Europe.)

Perhaps as many as one in ten world residents benefits from remittances sent home by workers abroad. In 2008, recorded remittances totaled $375 billion—well over three times the 2000 figure—and many people believe this is just a fraction of the aggregate funds sent back to countries of origin. Of the reported remittances, three-quarters ($283 billion) were sent to developing nations, and figure 2-10 portrays the regional distribution.

Sixty countries receive $1 billion or more annually in remittances. The four largest beneficiaries are India, China, Mexico, and the Philippines. Mexico attracted a reported $24 billion last year. The vast majority of these monies are spent on food, clothes, housing, education, and health, not on discretionary consumer goods. As the World Bank observes, "Allowing the freer flow of skilled and unskilled labor across national borders would probably do more to reduce poverty in developing countries than any other single policy or aid initiative."[10]

U.S. Labor Force

Over the past four decades, the primary drivers of America's labor force expansion have been absolute population growth (thanks heavily to immigration) and, as in so many parts of the world, increases in women's workforce participation. Nonetheless, annual labor force growth dropped to 1.6 percent in the 1980s and then to 1.1 percent in the 1990s. Between now and 2050, with baby boomer retirements, annual labor force expansion is projected to be just 0.6 percent.[11] Although this slower rate is of concern, America's total workforce will be growing, while Europe and East Asia will grapple with decline.

WOMEN

Gradually, the labor force participation rates of men and women have converged in America. According to the Population Reference Bureau (PRB), "In 1900, only 19 percent of women of working age were working or looking for work. In 2007, women represented

Figure 2-10

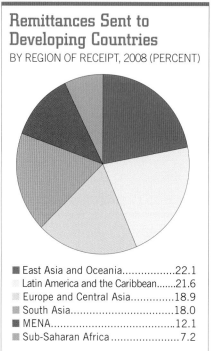

Remittances Sent to Developing Countries
BY REGION OF RECEIPT, 2008 (PERCENT)

- East Asia and Oceania.................22.1
- Latin America and the Caribbean.......21.6
- Europe and Central Asia..............18.9
- South Asia.................................18.0
- MENA...12.1
- Sub-Saharan Africa......................7.2

Source: World Bank estimates.

46 percent of people in the labor force."[12] A number of factors contributed to the evolutionary change:

▸ As the proportion of manual jobs decreased and that of white-collar positions grew, more opportunities became available to women.

▸ Improving wages offered a strong incentive for women to work. In 2006, women's median earnings were 77 percent of men's versus 64 percent in 1955.

▸ Rising divorce and separation rates forced women into the workforce.

▸ Greater control over the number and timing of children allows women to work around motherhood.

▸ Starting in the late 1980s, women have outnumbered men in college, and the disparity has widened steadily—to the point that 43 percent of women age 18 to 24 were in college in 2005 versus 35 percent of young men. Historically, women's college attendance has correlated with later marriages, fewer children, and greater workforce participation.

Women's participation in the labor force is currently 59.3 percent and is leveling off. Yet PRB analysts conclude "evidence from other developed countries suggests that the U.S. women's rate could move higher under the right mix of work-family policies."[13] Sweden offers a particularly strong model: thanks to broad societal support for parenting, its female participation rate is 61.3 percent. American women contribute about one-third of family income, so increasing their labor force involvement could be financially beneficial. As reported by Louis Uchitelle in *The New York Times*, "Only those families with a working wife have seen real improvement in their living standards."[14]

EDUCATIONAL ATTAINMENT

Education pays off in the workforce—for both women and men. According to the U.S. Census Bureau's 2007 American Community Survey, working adults with a master's, professional, or doctoral degree had median earnings of $61,287 in 2007, more than three times the $19,405 median for workers without a high school diploma. Just having a bachelor's degree resulted in income 2.4 times that of those who did not graduate from high school and 74 percent higher than those who finished their secondary educations.[15] A *Business Week* article points out, "According to the Bureau of Labor Statistics, 34 percent of adult workers in the United States now have a bachelor's degree or better, up from 29 percent ten years ago."[16]

RACIAL AND ETHNIC DIVERSITY

America's complex population mix is especially visible in the workforce because younger people are more racially diverse than were their parents' and grandparents' generations. By 2050, as reflected in figure 2-11, the Hispanic share of the labor force will nearly double to 24 percent, versus 13 percent in 2005. The Asian proportion will precisely double—from 4 percent in 2005 to 8 percent in 2050. Over the same time period, African Americans' share will move from 11 to 14 percent.

Figure 2-11

Distribution of U.S. Labor Force by Hispanic and Other Ethnicity

2005 (PERCENT)

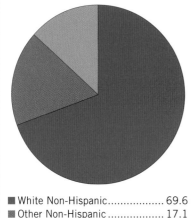

■ White Non-Hispanic.................. 69.6
■ Other Non-Hispanic 17.1
■ Hispanic................................. 13.3

2050 (PERCENT)

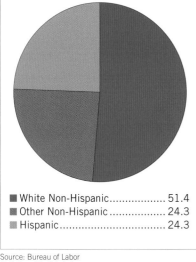

■ White Non-Hispanic.................. 51.4
■ Other Non-Hispanic 24.3
■ Hispanic................................. 24.3

Source: Bureau of Labor Statistics, *Monthly Labor Review*, November 2006.

In 2007, Hispanic men had the highest labor force participation rate of the three groups; however, at only 56.5 percent participation, Hispanic women had the lowest rate. African Americans registered the highest female participation (61.1 percent), followed by Asian women (58.6 percent). Participation among white women was virtually identical to that of Asian women.[17]

Another way of looking at the ethnic evolution of the United States labor force is demonstrated in figure 2-12. In the ten years from 2006 to 2016, 79 percent of the people leaving the labor force will be non-Hispanic whites, compared with only 56 percent of the new entrants. Hispanics will constitute 22 percent of new workforce members, compared with only 9 percent of those retiring.

FOREIGN-BORN WORKERS

Of America's 37.5 million foreign-born workers in 2006, more than half were from Latin America and another one-fourth were Asian. Because the two groups have radically different educational backgrounds, their skill sets also vary, as reflected in the fact that 46 percent of the Asian American workers were in professional jobs in 2006 versus 13 percent of the Latin Americans. As figure 2-13 illustrates, nearly six of ten workers born in South Central Asia (which includes India, Iran, Pakistan, and Bangladesh) are in professional occupations, and the same is true of half the East Asians (from China, Japan, South Korea, and Taiwan). Similarly, more than half the foreign-born workers from Canada and western Europe are professionals. In contrast, immigrants from Mexico and other Central American countries are least likely to be professional workers.

As highlighted in the box on America's scientists and engineers (see page 38), foreign-born residents are overrepresented in that workforce. Many are Asian. The United States

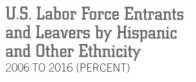

Figure 2-12

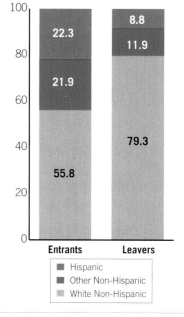

U.S. Labor Force Entrants and Leavers by Hispanic and Other Ethnicity
2006 TO 2016 (PERCENT)

Source: U.S. Bureau of Labor Statistics.

Figure 2-13

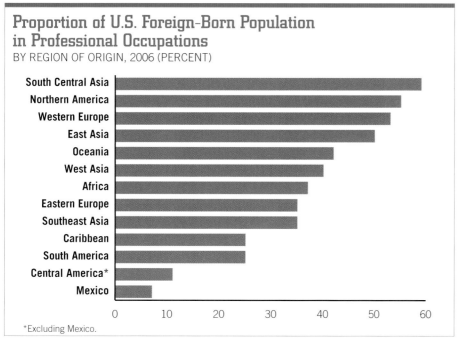

Proportion of U.S. Foreign-Born Population in Professional Occupations
BY REGION OF ORIGIN, 2006 (PERCENT)

*Excluding Mexico.

Source: Population Reference Bureau.

U.S. Science and Engineering Workforce

In 2006, America's 7.4 million engineers and scientists (including social scientists and technicians) accounted for 5 percent of the labor force. Despite their small proportion, these professionals are critical drivers of innovation, patents, and economic growth.

The metropolitan areas with the highest proportions and largest numbers of scientific and engineering workers are listed in the figure at right.

Approximately 19 percent of the science and engineering workforce is foreign born, a figure well above the 13 percent of America's overall population that was born elsewhere. In New Jersey, 37 percent of the science and engineering workforce is foreign born, just ahead of California's 36 percent. The proportion in Silicon Valley is an astounding 59 percent. Clearly, immigration and H-1B visas are important contributors to the maintenance of this workforce.

While foreign-born workers may be overrepresented among scientists and engineers, women are seriously underrepresented. Only 25 percent of this workforce is female, compared with 46 percent of the total U.S. labor force. More than half of all social scientists are women, but the shares of women among information technology workers and engineers are far lower. According to the PRB, "Recruiting more women into science and engineering will help offset the economic impact of aging baby boomers, many of whom are starting to reach retirement age."[18]

Scientists and Engineers by Metropolitan Area

Highest Percentage	Rank	Highest Number
San Jose	1	New York
Washington, D.C.	2	Washington, D.C.
Austin	3	Los Angeles
Seattle*	4	Chicago
San Francisco*	4	Boston
Baltimore**	5	San Francisco
Boston**	5	Dallas–Fort Worth
San Diego**	5	Philadelphia

*Tied for fourth.
**Tied for fifth.

remains a research and development powerhouse, but competition is increasing and many fear that America will not expand green card and H-1B visa issuance fast enough to accommodate the professionals needed to keep global firms competitive. Information technology and systems engineers are in particularly strong demand.

MANUFACTURING AND RETRAINING

Only 10 percent of America's workforce is employed in manufacturing, down from the peak of about 42 percent during World War II. In one industry after another, production and assembly have moved to offshore locations with lower labor costs. However, a modest reversal is occurring in select locations, thanks in part to a weaker dollar but also to strong labor productivity. David Rosenberg at Merrill Lynch, said that in 2008, "Unit labor costs, in dollar terms relative to the rest of the industrialized world, are the lowest in 30 years."[19] Prior to the recent economic downturn, both domestic and foreign producers were expanding in the United States in such diverse businesses as steel mills, farm equipment, medical supplies, ship- and boatbuilding, paperboard manufacturing, and chemical production.

A high proportion of today's manufacturing jobs are computerized and require skilled operators. America spends less than most industrialized countries on technical training and retraining, though with rapid technological evolution, skills are increasingly important. Both trade schools and community colleges are critical sources of technical education, but funding cutbacks restrain their ongoing operations, let alone expansion. In addition to adult workers needing retraining, the large Generation Y cohort is producing record numbers of young students; public schools are overwhelmed. As one example of problems in a sector with strong job growth, many community colleges have waiting lists for health care courses.

Real Estate Implications

Because underlying economic growth is essential for strong property appreciation, the size and capabilities of national labor forces are important investment considerations. Millions of people entered the labor force and moved out of poverty during the recent worldwide economic expansion, as opportunities for good jobs were created and workers moved to take advantage of them. Members of growing moderate- and middle-income households generate demand for retail, residential, and hospitality projects; service employment growth supports office development; and industrial expansion requires manufacturing and distribution facilities.

In the short term, rising unemployment will curtail consumer demand. Projections of joblessness in 2009 and 2010 are changing daily, not only in the United States but also worldwide. Although the economic slowdown appears to be hitting Europe even harder than the United States, the ultimate impact on developing nations is still uncertain. Most economists believe that GDP will continue to grow in Asia and Africa, albeit at a slower rate than in recent years.

Based on November 2008 forecasts from the International Monetary Fund, the global unemployment rate will rise to 6.1 percent in 2009, compared with 5.7 percent in 2007. The ILO's worst-case scenario is an unemployment rate of 7.1 percent, with 50 million more jobless people worldwide when compared with 2007's prosperity. The ILO's "probable" figure is a rise in unemployed persons of 30 million over the number in 2007. The effects will be profound for retailers, homebuilders, apartment owners, and developers and operators of leisure and travel-related facilities well into 2010.

Labor migration is important to real estate developers because construction laborers are often foreign: Mexicans in the United States, Nicaraguans in Costa Rica, Pakistanis in Dubai, and Romanians in Spain. With respect to project planning, development, finance and operations, the American real estate industry has two labor gaps, one visible now and one emerging:

▸ The skilled trades are not attracting enough young people: carpenters, sheet metal workers, electricians, mechanics, operating engineers, etc. Technical schools target new immigrants because young people born in the United States are not encouraged to work with their hands. The real estate industry should lobby for greater focus on this aspect of secondary and tertiary education.

▸ As the baby boomers begin to retire, the industry will lose management talent. The succeeding demographic group—Generation X—tended to bypass real estate because there were no entry-level jobs when they finished college during the industry's collapse in the early 1990s. By the late 1990s, dot.coms were more tantalizing than property companies. Thus, the industry lost a generation. Delayed retirements will be positive for many companies; current managers might hang around to see their projects and companies through the current crisis in order to stay busy, remain "in the mix," recover lost equity, or keep bread on the table.

Nice, France.

Consumer Income, | 3
Poverty, and Debt

Thriving economies maintain and expand their consumer bases—population and households, business entities, employees—and grow their purchasing power. As incomes rise in the developing world, moderate-income households can upgrade their shelter, move to permanent structures (with a lease or a mortgage), add more space, and enjoy safe drinking water and electricity. When poor families expand their buying power, demand increases for modern stores and shopping centers; successful entrepreneurs move from local, informal markets into shop spaces. Employment grows along the way.

Income Measurement

Analyzing consumer income, purchasing power, or consumption in the developing world is more complicated than estimating population. Among the difficulties:

▸ Much economic activity is informal, using cash or barter systems.

▸ National surveys are conducted infrequently.

▸ Income comparisons among nations or over time require adjustments for currency exchange rates, which fluctuate constantly.

▸ Because of local price variations, converting scant data on household earnings into dollars or euros can easily understate true purchasing power.

Estimates by the World Bank using 2005 data suggest that, on a purchasing power parity (PPP) basis, high-income countries generated 61 percent of global GDP, with 32 percent coming from middle-income nations and only 7 percent from poor countries. Without adjusting for differences in local purchasing power, high-income nations account for a 78 percent share.[1]

PER CAPITA INCOME

To arrive at a consistent way of comparing the relative affluence of countries across the globe, the World Bank and other international organizations use a standardized measure of national economic productivity—gross national income (GNI)—and then convert it to "international dollars" to arrive at PPP. GNI includes not only GDP but also the value of income transfers from abroad (such as remittances sent by citizens working overseas). An international dollar has the same purchasing power as the U.S. dollar within the United States, thus enabling comparisons of real price levels. To evaluate whether a country's national income growth is keeping pace with its expanding population, GNI PPP is divided by a commonly accepted population estimate to arrive at a per capita number. The result is a proxy for real purchasing power per person.[2]

Most—but not all—nations with high per capita GNI PPP are in the developed world. In 2007, Luxembourg topped the charts at $63,590, and 11 other European countries were in the top 20 (Norway, Switzerland, the Netherlands, Austria, Ireland, Sweden, Denmark, Belgium, Finland, Iceland, and the United Kingdom). The United States ($45,850) ranked sixth overall and fourth among countries with at least a million residents. Other affluent countries include oil-rich Middle Eastern nations (Kuwait, Bahrain) and Asian business centers (Singapore, Hong Kong, Japan). At the opposite end of the spectrum, countries with the lowest per capita GNI PPP are in sub-Saharan Africa, where economic growth has failed to keep pace with rapidly expanding populations.

The World Bank uses a second technique, the Atlas method, to classify countries as high, middle and low income, as shown in figure 3-1. The map demonstrates the limitations of using national economic productivity as a proxy for consumer purchasing power:

▸▸ Many countries classified as high income are rich in natural resources, but the income generated by resource extraction does not always trickle down to the majority of citizens. Equatorial Guinea is an example of a small (just over 500,000 people), oil-rich nation in central Africa

Figure 3-1

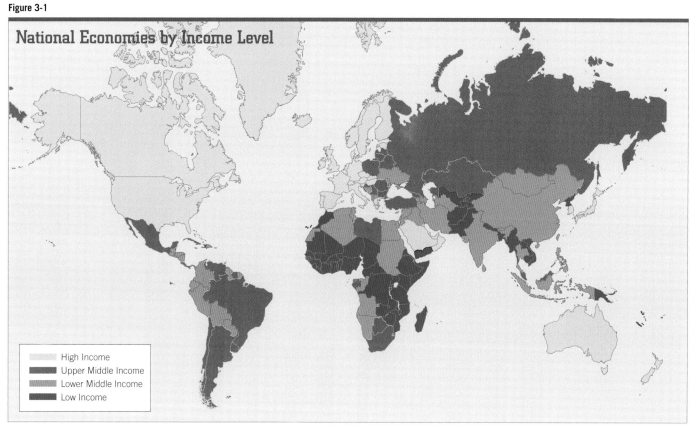

National Economies by Income Level

High Income
Upper Middle Income
Lower Middle Income
Low Income

Source: World Bank List of
Economies, July 2008.

where most families still eke out a living through subsistence farming. The *CIA Factbook* indicates that government officials and their family members own most businesses.[3]

» Nigeria is a large, oil-rich country that is classified as low income because its wealth is squandered and does not filter down.

» Numerous Caribbean islands are on the high-income list because they are havens for wealthy retirees from Northern America or Europe. Good jobs are scarce for the average Caribbean resident, and out-migration of young adults is the norm.

» With the exception of Haiti, all nations in Latin America and the Caribbean have economies that put them at least in the lower-middle-income group. Argentina, Brazil, Chile, and Mexico are classified as upper middle income.

» In the island nations of Oceania, those governed by developed nations (American Samoa, Guam, French Polynesia) have the highest incomes per capita; however, their spending powers do not begin to approach Australia's or New Zealand's.

» China and India, despite strong gains in GDP, have such large populations that per capita numbers still fall within the lower-middle-income range, as is also the case in most of Asia's other large nations (Indonesia, Iran, the Philippines, Thailand). Despite its importance in global politics, Pakistan is a low-income country, which undoubtedly contributes to its instability.

» Many nations with the highest incomes per capita are very small (Luxembourg, Qatar, Brunei, Kuwait) and have little influence on global buying power. Even Norway, which is rich in petroleum revenues, has fewer than 5 million people.

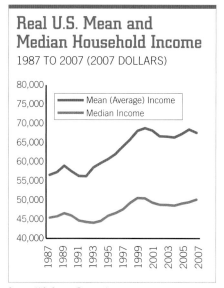

Real U.S. Mean and Median Household Income
1987 TO 2007 (2007 DOLLARS)

Source: U.S. Census Bureau, Income, *Poverty, and Health Insurance Coverage in the United States, 2007*, table A-1, p. 31.

HOUSEHOLD INCOME

Many countries prepare internal estimates of household income in their local currency, either as part of national census programs or in surveys of household earnings or consumption. Such data are useful for developers who are considering residential or retail investment or for retailers who are planning new store locations, because they reflect the actual spending power of local consumers.

These figures are typically available for small areas as well as for the nation as a whole. For example, information on household income (median, average, and distribution) can be obtained for metropolitan areas, counties, municipalities, census tracts, block groups, and even for customized geographies in the United States. Changes in mean and median U.S. incomes over the 20-year period from 1987 through 2007 are plotted in figure 3-2, expressed in constant 2007 dollars. Although real median household income increased between 1987 and 1999–2000, there has been little progress in the current decade. Because household sizes decreased over the 20-year period, however, well-being may have improved as the median income was spread among a smaller number of family members. Figure 3-2 also portrays average incomes as considerably higher than median incomes: very high earnings of small numbers of wealthy households skew the average, whereas median income expresses "typical" income levels.

Figure 3-3

The European Union's Mean and Median Disposable Incomes

(2006 EUROS)

Country	Mean	Median
Luxembourg	33,822	29,680
Iceland	31,630	27,989
Denmark	24,013	22,663
Ireland	23,360	19,679
United Kingdom	22,464	19,307
Finland	20,234	18,311
Austria	19,674	17,853
Sweden	18,694	17,730
Netherlands	19,376	17,260
Belgium	19,004	17,194
France	18,313	16,187
Germany	17,227	15,617
Cyprus	16,560	14,532
Italy	16,638	14,520
Spain	12,877	11,434
Greece	11,664	9,850
Slovenia	10,109	9,316
Malta	9,474	8,461
Portugal	9,550	7,311
Czech Republic	5,403	4,797
Hungary	4,582	3,847
Estonia	4,355	3,638
Slovak Republic	3,803	3,313
Poland	3,704	3,111
Latvia	3,230	2,534
Lithuania	3,055	2,532

Source: Eurostat.

Household Incomes in Australia

Australia's 2006 Census found that median household income was A$1,027 per week, up from A$782 in 2001—a nominal gain of more than 31 percent. In real dollars, Australia's median income grew by 13.2 percent, compared with a decline in the United States. In contrast to America's geographic income differences, there is little variation in median income among Australia's states and territories.

Figure 3-3 similarly compares mean and median incomes for nations in the European Union (EU) in 2006, expressed in euros. Luxembourg tops the list, followed by Iceland and Denmark. The least affluent EU countries are the former Soviet states in eastern Europe. Despite relatively low incomes, countries such as Poland and the Czech Republic have been the recipients of considerable investment in new retail space during the current decade—not because their populations were growing, but because their inventories of modern retail space were so scant.

In most developing countries, reliable household income numbers are hard to come by. Such figures as do exist fail to consider barter or work in the informal sector, which often makes up a larger economy than the formal, on-the-books economy. Translating varied national data across currencies poses further challenges.

INCOME INEQUALITY

Average income measures (such as per capita GNI or average household income) give no indication of how income is shared among households, both rich and poor. Economists commonly use the Gini coefficient to measure the extent to which a country's income is imperfectly spread among households at opposite ends of the income spectrum. A Gini coefficient of zero means that income is equally spread; in other words, the percentage of households in the highest income range would be identical to their share of aggregate household income. Households with incomes in the lowest 10 percent of the distribution would, in the aggregate, account for 10 percent of income. A coefficient of zero reflects perfect equality, and one indicates total inequality; no nation has a Gini score at either extreme. What is important is where a country falls on the spectrum.

In general, a nation with a coefficient of between 0.20 and 0.39 has a relatively even distribution of earnings. A coefficient of 0.60 or higher indicates high inequality, with affluent households garnering a disproportionate share of total household income. Countries that have published information on income inequality derive their Gini coefficients from national census surveys. (One limitation of the Gini coefficient is that it does not reveal exactly where the inequalities occur across income groups.)

To evaluate how income inequality changed in the recent period of prosperity and growth, the OECD commissioned a study of changes in income distribution and poverty rates among its member nations.[4] The results were mixed. Only two nations—Mexico and Turkey—showed a significant decrease in inequality, though modest improvements occurred in Greece, Ireland, the Netherlands, and the United Kingdom. Most countries showed no meaningful change in income distribution, but nine nations experienced an even greater concentration of income among the wealthiest households. Figure 3-4 shows Gini coefficients for European countries and the United States in 2006. A few conclusions from the OECD study:

▸▸ Over the past two decades, economic growth benefited high-income households more than it did the middle class and the poor. The income gap between rich and poor widened.

- A rise in inequality results when the rich improve their incomes relative to those of both low- and middle-income households.

- Income inequality in the United Kingdom is more widespread than in all other OECD countries with the exception of Italy and the United States. Well-paid workers in financial services contrast with low-wage immigrants from eastern Europe. Yet, both income inequality and poverty in the United Kingdom fell between 2000 and 2005, thanks to a combination of employment growth and social programs.

- Incomes are more equally distributed and fewer people are poor where social spending is high, as in the Nordic countries, Austria, Belgium, and the Netherlands.

- Key determinants of income inequality have been growth in the number of unemployed persons with limited skills or education, and a rising number of single-parent and single-person households.

- In most OECD countries, governments have increased spending on social benefits, in part to offset the trend toward greater income inequality. Had they not done so, the Gini coefficients would have risen more; however, the OECD sees social programs as having limited effectiveness in dramatically improving income inequality. More emphasis is needed on improving education and skills and expanding job opportunities—not easy tasks during a global recession.

- The United States has the greatest income inequality of the nations in figure 3-4, though Russia is close behind.

Russia's high-income households grew wealthier as oil, gas, and metals prices rose and foreign investment earnings increased. Between 2000 and 2007, the disposable income of households in Russia's top decile grew faster than that of any other income group, accounting for nearly 32 percent of total income in 2007, up from 25 percent in 1993. According to Euromonitor International, Russia's Gini coefficient rose from 0.29 in 1992 to 0.41 in 2007.[5]

Latin America has long been criticized for its split income profile: a few wealthy families and millions of peasants. Though improvement has occurred over the past 30 years, figure 3-5 shows that inequality remains at serious levels. Except for Uruguay, all the Gini coefficients in Latin America are higher than in the United States (which, at 0.46 in 2007, is notable itself).

EMERGING MIDDLE CLASS

Even in nations with high income inequality or a large percentage of low-wage workers, recent economic growth and changing demographics resulted in middle-class growth, as well as more affluent households. Middle-class gains occurred in nations as diverse as South Africa, Mexico, Ireland, and Poland. In China, increased income resulted from new manufacturing jobs; in India, information technology created white-collar and clerical job opportunities. In some countries, families' disposable incomes rose as remittances were sent home by relatives earning good wages abroad. Throughout eastern Europe, the shift to a market-based economy generated demand for consumer goods and better-quality

Figure 3-4

Income Inequality in European Nations, 2006

Country	Gini Coefficient
Sweden	0.23
Denmark	0.24
Slovenia	0.24
Austria	0.25
Czech Republic	0.25
Finland	0.26
Iceland	0.26
Netherlands	0.26
France	0.27
Germany	0.27
Belgium	0.28
Luxembourg	0.28
Malta	0.28
Slovak Republic	0.28
Cyprus	0.29
Spain	0.31
Ireland	0.32
Italy	0.32
United Kingdom	0.32
Estonia	0.33
Hungary	0.33
Poland	0.33
Greece	0.34
Lithuania	0.35
Portugal	0.38
Latvia	0.39
Russia	0.45
United States	0.47

Note: Countries with lower Gini coefficients have more equal income distributions.

Source: European Union, OECD.

Figure 3-5

Income Inequality in Selected Central and South American Countries

Country	Year	Gini Coefficient
Uruguay	2005	0.450
Venezuela	2005	0.476
Peru	2005	0.477
Argentina	2006	0.488
Costa Rica	2006	0.492
Mexico	2005	0.515
Dominican Republic	2006	0.519
Nicaragua	2005	0.523
Ecuador	2006	0.534
Paraguay	2005	0.539
Chile	2003	0.546
Honduras	2006	0.553
Colombia	2004	0.562
Brazil	2005	0.564

Note: Countries with lower Gini coefficients have more equal income distributions.

Source: Inter-American Development Bank.

housing. Growing exports of oil and other natural resources improved standards of living in nations throughout the Middle East, in Venezuela, and parts of Africa.

Each country's residents—and diverse global economists—have independent definitions of what constitutes "middle class":

▸▸ In a recent paper, the chief economist at Goldman Sachs suggested that about 70 million people a year are entering the middle class (defined as those with incomes between $6,000 and $30,000); and annual growth may reach 90 million by 2030.[6]

▸▸ The World Bank indicates that middle-class people have incomes of between $10 and $20 per day, adjusted for PPP, and predicts that the global middle class will total 1.15 billion by 2030. Developing nations, which were home to only 56 percent of the middle class in 2000, will account for 93 percent of its global population in 2030—with China alone constituting more than half the gain and India accounting for 12 percent.[7]

▸▸ The McKinsey Global Institute predicts that India's middle class will grow from 50 million to 583 million people over the next 20 years. Now the world's 12th largest consumer market, it will rise to number five. China's middle class—43 percent of the population in 2008—will account for 76 percent by 2025.

▸▸ Researchers at the Brookings Institution estimate that the ranks of the middle class will grow by 1.8 billion between 2008 and 2020, with one-third in China alone.

These projections all predate the recent drop in household asset values, which may make it difficult for households that recently achieved middle-class status to remain there.

Turning to the affluent, a recent *Wall Street Journal* article reported that the share of millionaires living in the United States is shrinking as wealth spreads to countries with rapidly growing economies, natural resource wealth, or both. The number of American millionaires grew 3.7 percent between 2006 and 2007; in contrast, such high-asset individuals increased by 19 percent (133,000) in Brazil, Russia, India, and China during the same period. Indian nationals account for four of the top eight slots on the *Forbes* billionaire list, and the number of Indian millionaires grew by 21 percent in 2006 and again by 23 percent in 2007.[8] Even so, the United States still has more millionaires (over 3 million) than any other country. The share of aggregate American household income earned by those in the top quintile is illustrated in figure 3-6. Though it rose from 44 percent in 1967 to 50 percent in 2007, there was little net change over the ten years from 1997 to 2007.

Poverty

At the other end of the spectrum, measures of poverty are closely tied to the issue of income inequality. Many countries have established their own poverty thresholds—usually based on a ratio of household income to median income—but the standards are not comparable across continents, let alone among countries. In the European Union, households are deemed poor if their incomes are less than 60 percent of median income; whereas in Latin America, the poverty threshold is defined as income that is less than half the median. In the United States, a household earning 60 percent of median income is considered to be low income; at 50 percent of area median income, such households are described as

Figure 3-6

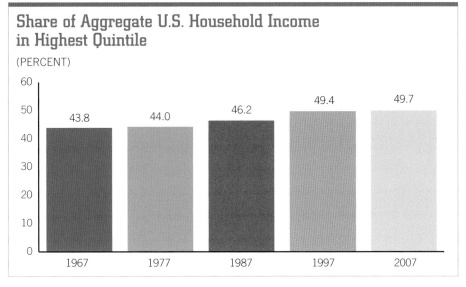

Share of Aggregate U.S. Household Income in Highest Quintile

(PERCENT)

- 1967: 43.8
- 1977: 44.0
- 1987: 46.2
- 1997: 49.4
- 2007: 49.7

Source: U.S. Census Bureau, *Income, Poverty, and Health Insurance Coverage in the United States, 2007*, table A-3, p. 41.

"very low" income (and are eligible for most subsidized housing programs), but they are not necessarily "poor" (see box on page 48).

The OECD report on inequality demonstrates a long-term trend: declining poverty rates among the elderly and rising poverty among children and young adults. A similar pattern can be seen in the United States, where the percentage of children living in poverty rose from 17 to 18 percent between 2006 and 2007—and stood eight percentage points higher than the poverty rate for senior citizens. In 2000, the gap in the poverty rate between children and the elderly was only six points.[9]

As discussed in chapter 1, 40 percent of global residents are living on the equivalent of less than $2 per day. In 2007, the ILO estimated that 487 million people could be classified as "working poor" using the $1 a day standard of poverty and nearly 1.3 billion using the $2 a day standard. The ILO concludes that the number of working poor is a product of the size of the labor force and the estimated national poverty rate, suggesting that all poor people of working age have to be employed to some extent in any country that lacks a social safety net.[10]

The ILO data in figure 3-7 demonstrate that the percentage of working people living in poverty is declining in every developing region; however, the number of poor people of working age is still on the rise in South Asia and sub-Saharan Africa. Lifting people out of poverty in populous, rapidly growing countries is a daunting task. Even nations that successfully lowered their poverty rates as their economies grew (most notably in India and China) continue to see increases in the number of poor people. Of course, the working poor are not limited to the developing world: half of all poor households cited in the OECD study of developed nations had at least some income from work, but either the jobs did not provide enough hours or the wages were too low to raise the laborer above the poverty level.

Poverty and poor housing conditions frequently go together. According to UN Habitat, one of every three urban residents in the developing world lives in a slum. By far the highest incidence is in sub-Saharan Africa, as shown in figure 3-8. Urban places that lack

Greater affluence helps retailers and apartment developers, but it can have unintended negative effects— more households buying automobiles raises demand for gasoline. Food prices go up as people can afford to eat more; "the average per capita consumption of meat in China, for example, has more than doubled since the mid-1980s. . . . A middle-class lifestyle in these countries, even if more frugal than what is common in rich nations, is more energy-intensive. . . . The demand (for electricity) in India will grow five-fold in the next 25 years. . . . The consumption patterns that an American, French, or Swedish family took for granted will inevitably become more expensive."

—Moses Naim,
"Middle Class Rising," p. A-7

Source: ILO, *Key Indicators of the Labor Market*, 5th edition, 2007.

Figure 3-7

Estimates of the Number of Working Poor in Developing Nations
WORKERS EARNING LESS THAN $2 A DAY

Number by Region (Millions)	1996	2006	Change
World	1,374.5	1,287.0	-87.5
Central and Southeast Europe (non-EU)	49.5	34.9	-14.6
East Asia	459.0	299.8	-159.2
Southeast Asia and Oceania	136.3	137.3	1.0
South Asia	433.7	469.0	35.3
Latin America and the Caribbean	65.4	60.6	-4.8
MENA	31.8	36.3	4.4
Sub-Saharan Africa	192.8	245.0	52.3
Share by Region (Percent)			
World	55	44	-11
Central and Southeast Europe (non-EU)	33	22	-11
East Asia	64	38	-26
Southeast Asia and Oceania	62	51	-11
South Asia	92	81	-12
Latin America and the Caribbean	34	25	-9
MENA	38	30	-8
Sub-Saharan Africa	88	86	-2

Note: 2006 estimates are preliminary.

Between 1981 and 2004, China "was able to lift more than 500 million people out of $1-a-day poverty, according to the World Bank. . . . While China has been successful in reducing poverty levels on a large scale, it has been unable to bridge the rising inequalities between rural and urban residents, which suggests that the benefits of economic growth have tended to favor urban populations."

—UN-Habitat, *State of the World's Cities: 2008/2009*, pp. 53–55

clean water, have limited sanitary services, house more than three persons per room, or lack durable structures can be classified as slums. Not all such neighborhoods have the full range of these problems, and many slums are electrified, have increasingly permanent buildings, have active residential rental and ownership markets, and accommodate small entrepreneurial businesses that, in aggregate, employ large numbers of people. Nonetheless, urbanization is drawing ever more poor people from rural areas to crowded slums—at a rate far outpacing the ability of governments or social service organizations to improve housing conditions.

Another corollary of poverty is malnutrition. In 2006, 13 percent of the world's population was undernourished (848 million people in total, of which 832 million were in developing nations). Countries with malnutrition rates exceeding 25 percent include North Korea, Mongolia, Cambodia, Bangladesh, Tajikistan, Haiti, Yemen, and numerous sub-Saharan African nations. There are African countries where less than 10 percent of the population is hungry (Mauritius, Ghana, Mauritania, Nigeria) and others where little progress has been made in reducing epidemic malnutrition.[11] Overall, 65 percent of the world's undernourished people live in just seven countries: India, China, the Democratic Republic of

Defining Poverty in the United States

Estimates of the number of poor households in the United States are based on income, as well as household size and the age of householder. For example, a household consisting of a single parent with two children needed to earn less than $16,705 in 2007 ($13,874 in 2000) to be considered poor. A single elderly person had to make less than $9,944, compared with $8,259 in 2000.

Poverty thresholds in the United States are not adjusted for geographic differences, which can be substantial: consider the differences in incomes and cost of living in New York City and rural Nebraska. Overall, 12.5 percent of Americans lived in households with incomes falling below official poverty thresholds in 2007.

Congo, Bangladesh, Indonesia, Pakistan, and Ethiopia. The ability to sustain nutritional improvements is affected by environmental conditions—drought or disease that reduces crop production—as well as by international market conditions that can drive up prices of basic food commodities, as was seen in early 2008. Escalating food prices[12] reduce household incomes, leaving fewer resources available for housing or other necessities. In wartorn nations, hunger is more prevalent now than it was in the early 1990s. Worldwide, an estimated 963 million people were said to be hungry in late 2008.

Household Debt

Economic well-being is affected not only by a household's income but by its ability to borrow money for major purchases—buying a home, a vehicle, household goods, or the equipment needed to start a business. In developing countries, government debt dwarfs household borrowing, and the vast majority of families have no access to credit. Hence the increasing attention given to microfinance programs that allow small farmers to buy seeds, animals, or equipment or enable urban dwellers to acquire supplies and produce goods to be sold locally or through export programs.

Over the past ten to 20 years, most wealthy nations experienced a rapid buildup in household debt, which is a double-edged sword. When economies are expanding, consumers borrow to purchase homes, cars, furniture, and other big-ticket items; however, when debt loads become burdensome (because of excess leverage or sudden declines in income), delinquencies and defaults climb. Lenders tighten credit standards, homebuilding slows, jobs are shed, families cut back on discretionary purchases, and retailers and shopping centers suffer.

Figure 3-8

Urban Population Living in Slums, by Region
2005

	Slum Population (Millions)	Share of Total Urban Population Living in Slums (percent)
Developing World	**810.4**	**36.5**
Sub-Saharan Africa	164.5	62.2
South Asia	201.2	42.9
East Asia	216.4	36.5
Southeast Asia	67.1	27.5
Latin America and the Caribbean	117.4	27.0
Oceania	0.5	24.1
West Asia (MENA)	31.3	24.0
North Africa (MENA)	12.0	14.5

Source: UN Habitat, *Global Urban Observatory*, 2008.

St. Lucia.

In the United States, annual household debt service as a percentage of disposable personal income rose from a low of 10.6 percent in 1980 to as high as 14.4 percent in most of 2006 and 2007. This ratio includes payments on mortgages and home equity loans, installment loans, and credit cards but does not include such other financial obligations as auto lease payments, rent, or property taxes. Total fixed obligations have exceeded 19 percent of disposable income for the past three years.

As credit became more readily available, Americans stopped saving, as shown in figure 3-9. The savings rate averaged less than 1 percent of disposable income from 2005 to 2008, compared with 7 to 8 percent in the first half of the 1990s. United States data for the second half of 2008 will show an uptick in the savings rate, as households worried about future job losses, held onto cash, and cut back on big-ticket purchases, entertainment, travel, and restaurant dining.

The United States was certainly not the only country in which consumer borrowing got out of hand. A similar pattern is evident in Canada, where household saving dropped from a high of 20.2 percent of disposable income in 1982 to 1.2 percent in 2005.[13] In Australia, net savings rates were actually negative from 2002 through 2006 as households spent down assets to pay expenses. In contrast, French, German, and Italian citizens saved more than 10 percent of disposable household income during the same period.[14] Figure 3-10 shows the multiple of total outstanding household debt to annual after-tax income for many OECD countries. It is interesting to note that the ratio of outstanding debt to income in the United States is far lower than that shown for Denmark, the Netherlands, New Zealand, Australia, and the United Kingdom. A few observations:

Changes in Credit Volume and Terms through the Decades

▸▸ In the 1920s, a typical American mortgage had a three- to five-year term but could be refinanced for up to 30 years. Long-term (30-year) mortgages did not exist until after World War II.

▸▸ A car loan in the 1920s required 40 percent down and had to be repaid in 12 months.

▸▸ In the 1930s, stores, gasoline stations, and hotels established credit accounts.

▸▸ Auto loan terms were extended to up to 30 months and housing downpayments were reduced to 25 to 30 percent in the 1950s. The first credit card that could be used at multiple establishments was issued.

▸▸ In the 1960s, half of all appliance purchases were made using installment loans. Visa and MasterCard first appeared.

▸▸ High interest rates dampened the growth of debt during the 1970s. Adjustable-rate mortgages were designed to compensate for high interest costs.

▸▸ Tax law changes in the 1980s favored mortgage debt over consumer credit. Home equity loans gained popularity.

▸▸ In the 1990s, auto loans stretched to 60 months or even longer.

▸▸ Two-thirds of college students now graduate with student loan debt, up from just half in the 1990s. The average student leaves college owing $20,000.

▸▸ Today's typical consumer has 13 credit obligations, including nine credit cards and four mortgages or installment loans.

▸▸ Forty percent of American households carry credit card balances, up from 6 percent in 1970. Average card balances per household exceed $8,500, an increase of almost 15 percent from 2000. Even so, a majority of households have no credit cards or pay off their balances every month. Forty percent have outstanding balances of under $1,000.

Sources: "The American Way of Debt," *New York Times* multimedia presentation, July 2008; www. myfico.com; Gretchen Morgenson, "Given a Shovel, Americans Dig Deeper Into Debt," p. A-1.

▶ Debt-to-disposable income ratios are imperfect measures; in countries with a larger public sector, tax burdens are higher and hence disposable income measures are lower. For such countries, especially Iceland and those in Scandinavia, a better indicator might be household debt as a percentage of GDP.

▶ As mentioned with respect to the United States, household debt measures do not include rent payments. Nations with a high percentage of renter households have lower debt-to-income ratios. Conversely, in countries where homeownership rose sharply over the last five years, debt ratios also increased.

▶ Total outstanding household debt in the United Kingdom reached 173 percent of disposable income in the first half of 2008, higher than the other G7 nations, including the United States. The savings ratio dropped to its lowest level since 1959, and disposable income was falling at the fastest rate since 1999.[15]

▶ House prices spiked dramatically in the United Kingdom, Spain, and Ireland, only to collapse in 2008, leaving many households with homes worth less than their outstanding mortgage debt.

▶ Aggregate household debt accounted for 66 percent of South Korea's GDP in 2007, up from 38 percent a decade earlier. Fortunately, three-fourths of South Korea's household debt is in mortgages; by law, loan-to-value ratios are much lower than those in the United States or Europe.[16] In contrast, though, the Korean government encourages the use of

Figure 3-9

Debt and Savings in the United States
2000 TO 2008

	Average Monthly Personal Saving Rate* (Percent)	Average Annual Household Savings (Dollars)	Average Debt Per Household (Dollars)
2000	2.37	2,032	76,927
2001	1.77	1,501	80,652
2002	2.36	2,042	87,666
2003	2.13	1,883	95,488
2004	2.07	1,897	103,820
2005	0.35	449	111,527
2006	0.73	376	118,080
2007	0.55	449	121,650
2008**	1.53	392	117,951

*Percentage of disposable personal income.
**Saving rate data for first 11 months; other data for first quarter of 2008.

Sources: U.S. Department of Commerce, Bureau of Economic Analysis; Amy Schoenfeld and Matthew Bloch, "The American Way of Debt," *The New York Times*, July 20, 2008, p. 15.

Figure 3-10

Total Household Debt as a Share of Annual Disposable Income
(PERCENT)

	1995	2000	2005
Denmark	188	236	260
Netherlands	113	175	246
New Zealand	96	125	181
Australia	83	120	173
United Kingdom	106	118	159
Ireland	—	81	141
United States	93	107	135
Sweden	90	107	134
Japan	130	136	132
Canada	103	114	126
Germany	97	111	107
Spain	59	83	107
France	66	78	89
Finland	64	66	69
Italy	32	46	59

— = not available.

Source: OECD, *Economic Outlook*, no. 80, p. 138.

credit cards, and merchants offer substantial discounts or rebates when cards are used. Half of consumption expenditures are paid with credit cards—one of the world's highest ratios—and South Korea ranks fifth in credit card spending per capita. The number of credit card terminals per million residents exceeds that of Japan by nearly 40 to 1.[17]

▶ Japan and Germany have kept debt under control; income gains outpaced household leverage between 2000 and 2005. Germany's unemployment rate has not spiked so far, and its retailers did well during the 2008 Christmas season when compared with the sales declines seen in the United States. Debt levels are higher, but stable, in Japan. Even so, both countries are vulnerable to a drop in export demand, as consumers in other countries cut back on purchases of luxury vehicles and electronics.

▶ South African government surveys in 2005 and 2006 suggest that 6.6 million households had some form of debt.

▶ Being in debt is considered shameful in some cultures, but this too is changing. Turkey now has more than 38 million outstanding credit cards, and credit card debt in 2007 reached nearly $18 billion, six times the 2002 level. The government set new laws limiting credit card marketing in 2006.[18] In traditional Muslim countries, new Islamic finance instruments allow families and businesses to "borrow" money without violating religious prohibitions against charging or paying interest.

▶ Many governments encourage the use of credit cards rather than cash, despite traditional taboos. The reason is simple: credit card transactions are recorded and can be taxed; cash sales are often lost in the underground economy. Credit card issuers see developing countries as an opportunity to increase market share—and profits.

Using Plastic Money

Two-thirds of the nearly 2.4 billion credit cards in circulation are held outside the United States. As shown in the figure, credit card ownership is widespread in Europe, Japan, Singapore, and South Korea, as well as in the largest South American countries, Thailand, Mexico, and Turkey. Note that the data refer to cards in circulation per capita—not per household. Between 2002 and 2007, card ownership grew most dramatically in Russia—by a factor of 20.

Credit card payments now exceed 6 percent of disposable income in Turkey, South Africa, Malaysia, and Venezuela. Other emerging economies are not far behind.

Source: Amy Schoenfeld, "What the World Owes," *The New York Times*, July 20, 2008.

Credit Cards per Capita
2007

More than 1.5	0.5–1.5	0.1–0.5	Under 0.1
Canada	Argentina	Austria	China
Denmark	Australia	Colombia	India
Japan	Belgium	Germany	Indonesia
South Korea	Brazil	Hungary	Philippines
United States	Chile	Israel	Russia
	Czech Republic	Malaysia	
	France	Mexico	
	Greece	Poland	
	Italy	Singapore	
	Netherlands	South Africa	
	Norway	Thailand	
	Portugal	Turkey	
	Spain	Venezuela	
	Sweden		
	United Kingdom		

Note: Data not available for all countries.

Source: *The New York Times*, from data provided by Euromonitor and Bloomberg. http://www.nytimes.com/interactive/2008/07/20/business/20debt-trap.html?ref=multimedia.

In mature economies, too-easy access to credit makes households vulnerable to economic downturns. In contrast, in emerging nations such as India, more sources of credit are needed if they are to create jobs for a growing population. Households—especially those in rural areas—do not have access to conventional credit sources. Borrowing from a moneylender (at very high interest rates) or from friends and family is far more common than borrowing from a bank or other nongovernment formal organization[19]—despite the growing presence of regulated microlenders.

Improving housing conditions in the developing world—and increasing the supply of new homes to meet the needs of a growing population—requires the creation of formal mortgage lending systems that involve both banks and government agencies.

Suria KLCC mall, Kuala
Lumpur, Malaysia.

Retail Globalization | 4

Globalization of retailing began with luxury French and Italian designer fashions at one end of the price point scale and American fast food and casual restaurant concepts (epitomized by Yum! Brands' Kentucky Fried Chicken and Pizza Hut, as well as McDonald's and Starbucks) at the other end. European grocery chains and hypermarkets (Carrefour, Auchan, SPAR) have been especially active, going beyond Europe to Latin America, the Middle East, Africa, and eastern Asia. America's version of hypermarkets—Super Wal-Mart, Target Greatland, Meijer—and warehouse clubs (Costco, Sam's Club, BJ's) have moved into United States suburbs and rural areas in a big way, but only Wal-Mart is a global player. Europe's traditional supermarket conglomerates that have purchased American grocery chains retain those chain's original names and store formats, so they operate behind the scenes.

European retailers are particularly active across international borders. Because their home bases often are small (the Netherlands), are intensely regulated (the United Kingdom), or have stagnant or shrinking populations (Germany), they need to expand elsewhere to build economies of scale with suppliers, cover corporate overhead, and generate good profit margins. The same factors affect Japanese and South Korean stores, which have sought locations elsewhere in Asia. In addition, Japanese specialty apparel and gift stores, cosmetic chains, and restaurants are scattered across the United States.

Typically, European apparel and specialty store chains expand first to neighboring countries and then branch out to Asia, South America, and the United States. New upscale malls in the Middle East's more affluent countries (Saudi Arabia, United Arab Emirates, Bahrain, and Turkey) offer attractive expansion opportunities.

Russia and China, because of their sheer size and the large numbers of new malls opened or under development, are attractive targets for global merchants and restaurant franchisors. For similar reasons, they have their eyes on India (where it is still difficult for foreign merchants to open multibrand stores) and Brazil. Forty percent of international retailers in a CB Richard Ellis survey (see box on page 56) say emerging markets are their strongest source of growth because of the expanding moderate- and middle-income populations and their attendant purchasing power.

For example, in terms of enclosed shopping center potential, Mexico is now where the United States was in the 1950s. Since 2005, the number of shopping centers with over 100,000 square feet has grown by 15 percent annually; and as of spring 2008, 80 malls

"While many retailers have taken their stores on the road, the industry remains far less global than many comparable consumer-oriented businesses. Think about the leading companies in consumer products, hospitality, food service, telecommunications, and entertainment. These industries are far more global than retailing, with the leading players achieving a much higher share of revenue and profits from outside their home markets than is true of retailing."

—Ira Kalish, *Revisiting Retail Globalization*, Deloitte Research, December 2008, p. 1

IMAX CORPORATION

An IMAX theater in Latin America.

were under construction around the country. The concept of a shopping center—in which an operating owner takes care of security, maintenance, parking, coordinated hours, etc.—is a new phenomenon in Mexico, where malls provide high entertainment as well as retail value. Moderate- and middle-income families spend entire weekend days inside air-conditioned malls, going to movies, patronizing knowledge-based gaming facilities, assembling at the large food courts, sending children on train or other rides within the centers, and shopping. Patrons are willing to pay for mall parking, which is guarded and therefore safe.

Clothing and accessory stores catering to teens and young adults have been particularly active in global expansion, as seen in figure 4-1. Chains move across borders in Europe and also to the Americas (including relatively poor countries in Central America), the Middle East, and Asia. Though initially lucrative, such expansions are fraught with difficulty. The number of teenagers in Europe is stagnant to declining, and the fashion tastes and shopping habits of 12- to 24-year-olds are notoriously fickle. The shelf life of new concepts, even with modest prices, can be short—witness Mexx's closing of its U.S. and U.K. stores and the declining fortunes of Old Navy. Spain's Zara, which sells apparel and accessories, has made a conscious decision to keep its clothing manufacturing operations at home or in nearby Portugal so it can respond quickly to shopper whims and keep styles fresh.

Opportunities and Obstacles

Despite important differences among countries and between basics (food) and fashion, a focus on emerging markets is considered a defensive strategy for retailers during the current period of economic contraction in the United States, Canada, Europe, and Japan. Consulting firm A. T. Kearney suggests:

Retail Chains Expand across Borders

Countries with the Most International Retailers
(PERCENT)

	Share of International Retailers with a Presence
United Kingdom	55
Spain	51
France	49
Germany	47
Italy	45
Switzerland	42
Austria	42
United Arab Emirates	41
China	40
Russia	39
United States	39
Netherlands	38
Singapore	38
Belgium	37
Ireland	35

In a 2008 survey, "How Global is the Business of Retail?" CB Richard Ellis found that 90 percent of store chains had a presence in at least one country outside their domicile. However, only 15 percent of survey respondents could truly be labeled "global retailers"—having a presence in 30 or more countries. Luxury chains—mostly French and Italian designers selling apparel, shoes, accessories, and other fashion items—had the largest global presence. Such stores, with their well-known brands and high profit margins, can establish a presence by opening a single "High Street" flagship location. Stores serving the middle market or chains catering to teenagers and young adults need more locations to justify advertising and logistics costs. Department stores seem to have the greatest difficulty moving to new markets: only 5 percent of those surveyed had locations in more than ten countries. Stores based in an EU country have the easiest time "going global" because they have so many proximate countries.

Source: CB Richard Ellis, *"How Global is the Business of Retail?,"* 2008, p. 4; based on a survey of 226 retail chains with international operations.

Even when faced with tough economic conditions in their home markets, [retailers] can realize continued double-digit same-store sales growth and profits in their emerging markets. . . . Pursuing expansion into new markets appears to be the best means to further diversify their customer and operations bases. . . . It will allow them to muscle through the current economic turmoil and become truly differentiated from the competition.[1]

Countries with the greatest promise have strong GDP growth, young populations (that spend a higher percentage of income on goods and services), logistics facilities to handle imported goods, limited organized competition, and public policies favorable to imported products and foreign direct investment. Initially, at least, most global retailers need local partners. Franchising is a relatively quick way to establish a store's identity in a new market. Corporate-owned stores are often introduced later, once the chain and its goods are known and accepted in the marketplace. Retailers who want to "go global" must overcome significant hurdles:

▶ Language barriers in advertising;

▶ Currency fluctuations and inflation;

▶ Need for bilingual or multilingual management;

▶ Differences in business operating styles and employee expectations;

▶ Lack of modern shop space and supply chain infrastructure;

▶ Legal requirements, including local regulations that limit store sizes and national regulations on foreign ownership or franchising;

▶ Cultural differences that affect merchandising;

▶ Poorer shoppers' desire to buy in small, affordable quantities on a daily or weekly basis;

▶ Unique employment regulations; and

▶ Limitations on profit repatriation.

Local shopping patterns change slowly. For example, the developing world's reliance on open-air markets selling produce, fish, meats, and other daily necessities is not easily

Figure 4-1

Mid-Market Apparel Stores: A Global Sampler

Chain Name	Country of Origin	Global Locations
Bench	Philippines	China, Guam, United Arab Emirates, United States
Cotton On	Australia	Hong Kong, New Zealand, Singapore
H&M	Sweden	Canada, China, Czech Republic, Egypt, Greece, Italy, Japan, Poland, Saudi Arabia, Slovak Republic, Slovenia, United States, and throughout northern and western Europe; over 21,500 stores in 33 countries
Lululemon	Canada	Australia, Hong Kong, United States
Mango	Spain	Australia, Canada, France, Germany, Hong Kong, Italy, Japan, United States
Mexx	Netherlands	Canada, Guatemala, Hong Kong, United Arab Emirates, and throughout Europe; 351 stores and 72 outlets
Next	United Kingdom	Bahrain, China, Cyprus, Czech Republic, Denmark, Egypt, Gibraltar, Hong Kong, Hungary, Iceland, India, Indonesia, Ireland, Japan, Jordan, Kuwait, Lebanon, Macau, Oman, Pakistan, Poland, Qatar, Romania, Russia, Saudi Arabia, Turkey, Thailand, Slovak Republic, United Arab Emirates, Ukraine
Uniqlo	Japan	China, France, Hong Kong, South Korea, United Kingdom, United States
Who AU	South Korea	United States
Zara	Spain	Argentina, Chile, Colombia, Cyprus, Dominican Republic, Egypt, El Salvador, Honduras, Hong Kong, Indonesia, Israel, Japan, Jordan, Lebanon, Malaysia, Mexico, Morocco, Oman, Panama, Philippines, Qatar, South Korea, Thailand, Tunisia, Turkey, United States, and throughout Europe; 1,500 stores total

Sources: Retailer Web sites.

supplanted by indoor, climate-controlled supermarkets or specialty stores, especially in remote locations. Yet shoppers in the developing world typically support modern retail alternatives when they become available. Thanks to global communication, they know about global brands and want to own them. Also, in places like South Africa, malls are anchored by supermarkets, so frequent visits are encouraged—to create the same habit as going to traditional market stalls.

Labor Issues in Retailing

Retailers that are expanding across borders begin by sending experienced home-country management to new locations, but they recruit and train indigenous managers and sales staff fairly quickly. Countries with young and well-educated labor forces have an advantage in attracting stores. In both developed and emerging markets, retailers compete with other industries that offer higher wages or better career opportunities. At the same time, retail clerks and food and beverage workers do not need college educations, so these are good jobs in developing countries. Employers have to provide effective training programs, but the payoff can be a cadre of proud and loyal employees.

In its 2007 Global Retail Development Index, management consulting firm A. T. Kearney noted that India, Russia, and China face labor challenges, with an acute shortage of middle and senior retail management, especially in second-tier cities, where expansion efforts are currently focused. The firm ranked emerging countries based on a variety of labor, demographic, and economic indicators, concluding that the top five emerging retail markets based on labor factors were Malaysia, the Slovak Republic, Thailand, India, and Chile. Important in Malaysia's top ranking was its high literacy rate, well-regarded education system, and young labor pool.[2]

In the United States, looming retirements of experienced executives and managers could pose problems over the next decade for shopping center owners and managers and their store tenants. Generation Y members entering the industry will introduce new ways of conducting business and communicating—with one another, bosses, and customers. Such changes are inevitable, but generational conflicts may arise between younger boomer and Generation X managers and their Generation Y employees.

China

With over 1.3 billion residents, more than half of whom live in urban areas, China's market potential is huge. An impressive percentage of its population has moved from low to moderate and even middle incomes over the past 15 years, so Chinese households have experienced a vast increase in purchasing power. The government eagerly allowed Western store chains into the nation, partly because domestic manufacturing focused on generating goods for export, not for sale to Chinese consumers. Global retailers and experienced shopping center owner/developers responded, almost always in joint ventures with Chinese entrepreneurs. Early activity concentrated in the big metropolitan areas (Beijing, Shanghai, Guangzhou) with the most affluent and sophisticated consumers. Chinese yuppies value global brands—as an easy way to demonstrate their participation in the larger world. They

American retail trade accounts for just over 11 percent of total nonfarm jobs, with another 7 percent of persons employed at restaurants and drinking places. In the United States, the 2007 median hourly wage for a grocery store cashier was only $8.36, with $9.18 for grocery stock clerks, $8.72 for sales personnel in clothing stores, and $16.04 for their first-line managers.

—U.S. Bureau of Labor Statistics

are avid shoppers, enjoy socializing in malls (including at Starbucks, where they drink almost as much coffee as tea), wish to visit Hong Kong to shop, and are generally aspirational buyers.

Because the government provides little in the way of social safety nets for retirement, health care, or education, typical Chinese households—and especially urban ones—are notoriously high savers. Their behavior has been exactly opposite to that of American households over the past several decades. As both countries deal with the effects of the recession, American consumers will be saving more while Chinese shoppers will increase their spending. As China's leaders reexamine their export-based economy and adopt more of India's inward approach of catering to their own enormous population, greater encouragement of consumerism may follow.

Retail developers have transitioned to second-tier Chinese cities, where modern space is still lacking. Experienced mall managers from Singapore, Japan, and Korea see China as a place to expand their portfolios. As shopping center development becomes widespread, not all projects are successful. The most notorious failure is the huge South China Mall in Dongguan, which opened in 2005 with over 7 million square feet of space. The European-themed megamall was designed for 1,500 tenants that never materialized: its location was not accessible by transit, competitive centers were well established, and area residents were factory workers with modest incomes. The project is being redeveloped.

Other Asian countries are learning from China's experiences in retail development. In 2008, Vietnam was ranked as the top emerging market for retail by A. T. Kearney. Another analyst noted, "Vietnam is at the nascent stages of development and moving at high speed. . . . Vietnam will leapfrog China's retail revolution by going straight from the mom-and-pop shops to the shopping center phase, skipping the department store phase altogether."[3]

India

India's enormous, increasingly affluent population is another tempting target. By some estimates, the middle class totals at least 300 million people (the population of the entire United States) and by other estimates, closer to 600 million. In 20 years, the middle-class population has grown eightfold. Even so, offshore retailers are few and far between in India; foreigners are permitted to hold a controlling interest only in stores that sell a single brand. Another deterrent is high import taxes. Through wholesaling, foreign companies can be involved in consumer-oriented business in India. For example, Indian conglomerate Bharti has a 50/50 joint venture with Wal-Mart. Bharti runs the stores, and Wal-Mart handles the logistics.

Upscale hotels in India's major business cities have high-end foreign boutiques, but European hypermarkets and department stores are noticeably absent. The retail landscape is filled with small vendors, family operations, and Indian retail conglomerates that wield considerable political clout and strongly oppose interlopers' proposals.

Although branded stores in malls make up only 4 percent of the Indian retail market,[4] aggressive shopping center development is underway. Ten years ago, there were no American-style shopping centers; 300 to 500 are predicted by 2010, if they are not sidelined by the recession. Tenants can be found among the many chains operated by Indian conglomerates such as Pantaloon Retail. Headquartered in Mumbai, the company operates over 12 million square feet of retail space, has in excess of 1,000 stores across 71 cities in India, and employs upward of 30,000 people. Among its stores are Pantaloons (apparel), Big Bazaar (hypermarkets), Food Bazaar (supermarkets), Home Town (home furnishings), Collection I (furniture), and eZone (consumer electronics).

Cultural differences also affect demand. Many older women who prefer the comfort of traditional saris and sandals rather than international fashions tend to shop frequently in neighborhood stores (kiranas) instead of patronizing distant malls. Seven in ten Indians still live in rural areas, making it difficult to operate large stores successfully outside of major cities.

India will not be unscathed by the global recession and credit constriction. One of the largest grocery chains, Subhiksha Trading, shuttered its 1,600 stores and laid off its entire staff when plans for an IPO fell through and credit could not be secured.

Europe

As international real estate consulting firm King Sturge summarizes, "Europe represents a combination of more than 30 different countries, each with a distinct culture, contrasting macroeconomic drivers and rates of retail sales growth, varying levels of existing retail supply, and different planning regimes."[5] The International Council of Shopping Centers (ICSC) defines a modern European shopping center as a retail property that is planned, built, and managed as a single entity, with a minimum gross leasable area of 5,000 square meters (53,820 square feet). Nearly a quarter of European retail sales (500 billion in 2006) were said to be generated at shopping centers, whether enclosed or open-air, with consumers spending

Amsterdam, Netherlands.

DEBORAH BRETT

Figure 4-2

Sources: ICSC, DTZ Research, Cushman and Wakefield.

Shopping Center Space in Europe
YEAR END 2007 (SQUARE METERS PER 1,000 RESIDENTS)

<100	100–200	200–300	300–600	>600
Bulgaria	Czech Republic	Austria	Ireland	Norway
Croatia	Germany	Denmark	Luxembourg	
Greece	Hungary	Estonia	Sweden	
Romania	Italy	Finland	Netherlands	
Russia	Latvia	France		
Slovenia	Lithuania	Portugal		
Ukraine	Poland	Spain		
	Slovak Republic	Switzerland		
		United Kingdom		

an annual average of €1,110 per capita. The continent had an estimated 5,700 centers as of 2007, totaling 111 million square meters (1.19 million square feet) of leasable area.[6]

Yet the European shopping center industry is still relatively small when compared with that of Northern America. Europe had only 0.226 square meters (2.4 square feet) of shopping center space per capita in 2007,[7] compared with nearly ten times as much (22.4 square feet) in the United States. and 13.7 square feet in Canada. As seen in figure 4-2, however, the overall average for Europe masks considerable differences in supply among individual countries, reflecting the evolution of the retail landscape:

▸▸ Western Europe had a plentiful supply of stores, albeit in small shops housed in "High Street" business districts. Consumers made frequent trips to the store, often on foot or by public transportation. As people relocated to the outskirts of metropolitan areas they became more reliant on cars, and municipalities looked favorably on shopping center developments at the urban fringe as a way to move traffic off crowded narrow streets.

▸▸ By contrast, retail space in the former Soviet bloc was scarce and lacking in amenities. With increasing affluence, eastern European consumers wanted a better array of goods and more pleasant—even exciting—shopping and entertainment environments. According to the European Shopping Centre Trust, 130 new projects were planned for eastern Europe (not including Russia) between 2006 and 2009, doubling the existing stock. Development has been widespread in Poland, the Czech Republic, and Slovenia.

▸▸ Sweden, Norway, the Netherlands, and the United Kingdom have at least double the average European amount of shopping center space per capita. Countries in southeastern Europe and the Balkans fall well below the average, though some are catching up. In its recent *Market View* for central and eastern Europe, CBRE suggests that shopping center stock in Bulgaria, Croatia, Romania, and the Slovak Republic will increase rapidly over the next few years, while Ukraine and Serbia will lag behind.[8] With the exception of Hungary, economic growth in eastern Europe will continue, albeit at a slower pace than in recent years.

Russia's recent "petro prosperity" strengthened demand for luxury goods, entertainment, and dining space, but its Soviet-era building inventory did not offer suitable venues. In the early years after the fall of communism, land ownership issues were understandably murky, so it took time to launch serious new construction. As in China, Russia's shopping center developers focus on large vacant tracts at the urban perimeter and on redevelopment sites in Moscow and Saint Petersburg, with vertical, mixed-use, supermarket-anchored projects receiving the greatest attention. At this point, the big metropolitan markets are nearing saturation; however, between 2008 and 2010, an estimated 54 million retail square feet are expected to be completed in Russia.

Attention is shifting to provincial cities with populations over 1 million. U.S. real estate investment trust Developers Diversified is interested in building three malls a year in Russia and neighboring Ukraine, focusing on secondary cities. An IKEA-anchored center in Novosibirsk received a great deal of press attention, and another store is opening in Rostov-on-Don.[9] Additional IKEA stores are planned in Krasnodar and Samara. Auchan and other large European chains have been active in Russia, and despite earlier problems in Germany, Wal-Mart is said to be interested.

After Russia, Poland is the busiest retail market in eastern Europe. The combination of size and relative lack of modern space has turned Poland into a magnet for global retailing in apparel, groceries, and general merchandise—and for developers. Tesco alone has over 300 supermarkets. According to Jones Lang LaSalle, more than a million square meters (10.8 million square feet) of shops were planned for opening in 2008, up from just 205,000 square meters (2.2 million square feet) in 2007. Despite its large construction pipeline, Cushman and Wakefield estimates that Poland has less than 1.5 square feet of shopping center space per capita.

Grocery Wars

Fierce price competition is underway between traditional supermarket chains and hard discounters (notably Aldi and Lidl, both based in Germany). Global prices for wheat, corn, oil, and other staples skyrocketed in early 2008 as farmers dealt with higher fuel and fertilizer costs and weather-related issues (drought in Australia, typhoons in Southeast Asia). Although commodity prices moderated later in the year, the cost of food products did not come down, because producers were locked into expensive long-term contracts.

Financially strapped shoppers are turning to two ways of beating increased grocery prices: shopping at discount markets and buying private-label brands. Hard discounters offer fewer items (900 to 1,600 SKUs compared with 20,000 in large markets). At Aldi stores (also represented in low- and moderate-income U.S. neighborhoods), known brands account for only 5 to 7 percent of products offered, compared with 25 to 35 percent at Lidl, another chain based in Germany. Leader Price is capturing a growing share of grocery purchases in France, where hypermarkets have held a virtual monopoly for many years and food prices are higher than in neighboring Germany. The share of the grocery euro captured by hard discounters in 2007 was estimated at 20 to 30 percent in Austria, Germany, and Norway, but only 5 to 15

percent in France, Italy, and Spain. In the United Kingdom, discounters capture an astounding 45 percent.

Grocery chains are offering more private-label goods, which have lower price points than name brands and generate higher margins for the stores. U.K.-based Tesco now offers four private label brands at different price points. Store brand food accounts for only 16 percent of U.S. sales (compared with 22 percent in Europe), but the U.S. volume increased by 10 percent in 2008. Interestingly, Wal-Mart sells relatively few private-label items, preferring to keep prices low through hard bargaining with suppliers. But it, too, is climbing on the private-label bandwagon.

Industry observers suggest that food demand patterns are changing, with an increasingly affluent global population consuming more grains and meat than ever before. Despite recent price increases, shoppers in developing nations remain much more wary of off-brands.

Sources: Christina Passariello et al., "Europe Eats on the Cheap," *Wall Street Journal*, September 30, 2008; Matthew Boyle, "Slugfest at the Supermarket," *Business Week*, February 9, 2009; Justin Lahart et al., "Consumers Cut Food Spending Dramatically," *Wall Street Journal*, February 13, 2009, p. B1; Cecile Rohwedder, "Tesco Broadens Discount Line as Retailers Fight for Shoppers," *Wall Street Journal*, February 13, 2009, p. B2; "The Germans Are Coming," *The Economist*, August 10, 2008, p. 61; Euromonitor.

Although Germany is the second largest country in Europe after Russia and is home to many of the continent's big grocery retailers, it is only the third retail market—behind France and the United Kingdom. Unlike most European countries, Germany did not experience a retail construction frenzy: developers were cautious because of the declining population (see chapter 5) and its reputation for saving, not spending. Consequently, Germany may be better positioned to weather the current downturn.

Throughout Europe, new retail space is an important part of urban redevelopment projects, where vertical shop space is combined with modern office space and hotel rooms. Shops and restaurants are also being added when airport terminals are modernized, providing better service to the millions of travelers vacationing in Europe or changing planes on their way to other destinations worldwide.

Outdoor stall near Tangier, Morocco.

The Middle East

With so much attention given to the construction of exotic retail space in Dubai, market analysts have overlooked the fact that populous Egypt is the region's most understored country. The ICSC reports that three dozen malls are operating in Cairo and its suburbs, and another dozen in the port city of Alexandria. A. T. Kearney's index of global retail development ranks Egypt as the number-five emerging market.[10] For years, regulations were hostile to imported consumer staples in general and luxury goods in particular, but retailers now represented in Egypt include Carrefour, Metro supermarkets (Germany), and the Turkey-based Beyman department store. Other Middle Eastern and North African nations ranked in the top 15 emerging countries for retail opportunity include Morocco, Saudi Arabia, Turkey, and Algeria.

With its increasingly affluent and relatively young population, Turkey has attracted considerable interest from domestic and foreign developers and international retailers. American retailers favor Turkey more than any other individual emerging market, according to a recent survey by CB Richard Ellis. Respondents cited the ease of foreign ownership as well as the country's economic stability. Turkey was ranked third by Asian retailers and by stores selling luxury goods. Overall, 15 percent of the CBRE retailers said they had either opened their first store in Turkey in 2007 or were actively looking there.[11]

United States

Earlier in this decade, America's housing boom fueled growth in retail sales for furniture, decorative items, flat-screen TVs, and appliances. Households that were not trading up to larger, more expensive homes were spending money on room additions, renovations, and repairs and were generating strong same-store gains for home improvement centers. Long working hours meant more restaurant meals and greater demand for gourmet takeout food. Consumers spent more on entertainment, ranging from movie tickets to sporting events to Broadway shows. The older baby boomers were in their peak earning years, and both inflation and unemployment were low. With the sudden downturn in the economy and the consequent decline in sales at virtually every type of retailer, it is important to take a look at broader trends that will outlast the current recession.

DEMOGRAPHIC CHANGES

Changes in household characteristics and recession-related declines in disposable income are already changing spending and saving habits in response to the economic downturn:

▸▸ As the first half of the big-spending baby boom generation ages beyond the peak earning years, it is uncertain how they will respond to diminished financial resources. With retirement savings in freefall, many boomers will remain in the workforce longer—of necessity.

Figure 4-3

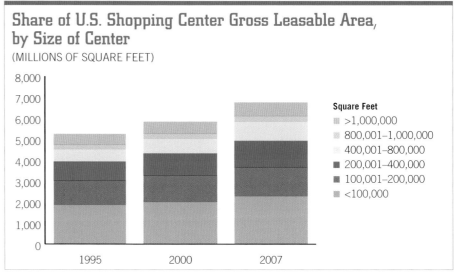

Share of U.S. Shopping Center Gross Leasable Area, by Size of Center
(MILLIONS OF SQUARE FEET)

Square Feet
- >1,000,000
- 800,001–1,000,000
- 400,001–800,000
- 200,001–400,000
- 100,001–200,000
- <100,000

Source: International Council of Shopping Centers, "Trends in the Shopping Center Industry," *Retail Real Estate Business Conditions*, vol. 5, no. 15, May 16, 2008.

- Eco-conscious Generation Y members will ask themselves if they need so many "things."

- More single-person households will generate demand for smaller homes and condominiums, which need less furniture and fewer decorative items.

- With an ever-growing foreign-born population—and continued interest in ethnic foods and clothing among second-generation consumers—retailers will still need to tailor their merchandise mix to the local population. Watch for more Asian and Hispanic markets, and more shelf space devoted to ethnic foods in traditional stores.

FEWER ENCLOSED MALLS

Although neighborhood and community centers continued to be built in areas experiencing recent household growth, developers have created very few enclosed superregional malls in the United States—in stark contrast with what happened in Europe, China, and the Middle East over the past five years. The difficulties of building new enclosed malls have been well understood for years—the lack of large, suitable sites; years of advance planning; lengthy (and often acrimonious) public approval processes; and multiyear construction. What changed over the past decade was the disappearance of full-line department store chains that served as anchor tenants. Many went out of business; others merged—to the point that mall developers found it impossible to fill four or more anchor spaces. Just 13 malls larger than 700,000 square feet were scheduled to open in 2008 and 2009, and only one of those was enclosed. All but two of the large new shopping centers are located in growing Sunbelt states; many metropolitan areas simply do not need any more regional mall space.

As figure 4-3 suggests, the percentage of total shopping center space in malls with more than 800,000 square feet has been declining. Rather than focus on new construction, owners and managers of enclosed regional and superregional malls in the United States are renovating their properties to keep them fresh and competitive, and looking for successful store chains and new concepts to fill vacant spaces.

Supplanting regional malls in construction volume is the open-air lifestyle center, with its lower occupancy costs and greater visibility for small tenants. The past decade has also seen a renaissance in retail and entertainment activity in urban and suburban downtowns and in neighborhood business districts. Although a far larger share of retail activity in the United States takes place in shopping centers (54 percent) than is the case in other countries, eclectic business districts are still very much alive (see figure 4-4).

TENANT MIX CHANGES

In the past, clear tenant distinctions existed among shopping center types, but definitions are blurring today. For example, urban street retail—once the province of independent entrepreneurs or small regional chains—now draws national chains that used to locate only inside regional malls. Enclosed malls have evolved as well. With so many stores going out of business or vacating spaces that no longer meet their locational requirements, chains that might not have taken space in a regional mall ten years ago are giving them a second look. Increasingly, vacant department stores are being subdivided and retenanted with bookstores, home furnishings, movie theaters, and other store types—often with

Source: International Council of Shopping
Centers, "Trends in the Shopping Center
Industry," *Retail Real Estate Business Conditions*,
vol. 5, no. 15, May 16, 2008.

Figure 4-4

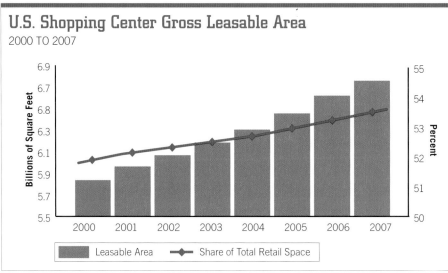

U.S. Shopping Center Gross Leasable Area
2000 TO 2007

entrances directly accessible from parking lots. Rents are often lower than would be the case if these tenants went to brand-new centers. Another example is the addition of open-air strips at the perimeter of superregional malls, providing space for new apparel, restaurant, and entertainment attractions not found inside.

CONSUMERS RETRENCH

In the fourth quarter of 2008, American shoppers suddenly put the brakes on conspicuous consumption. Consumer confidence, as reflected in the Reuters/University of Michigan monthly survey, plummeted in October and made only scant gains in the following two months. (See figure 4-5.) The January 2009 index, at 61.2, was substantially below the 78.4 registered a year earlier and the cyclical peak of 96.9 reached in January 2007. Survey analysts said,

> *Consumers have become defensive minded, protecting their future living standards through increased saving, even if it meant giving up some items, changing brand preferences or spending habits. . . . The majority of consumers reported in January that their financial situation had worsened. . . . Consumers were hesitant to make large purchases due to their heightened uncertainty about their future job and income prospects, even though most consumers thought that current prices were quite attractive across a broad range of household products, including vehicles.[12]*

Signs of a weakening economy were evident earlier in 2008—rising unemployment and housing foreclosures acting as the canaries in the coal mine—but the recent sales tumble affected virtually all components of the retail sector. The list of defunct store chains keeps growing (although many were in trouble long before 2008 drew to a close), while others are shuttering underperforming locations. At the same time, retailers are approaching landlords to renegotiate existing lease terms or seek significant rent reductions at renewal time. Landlords are also vulnerable to cotenancy clauses, putting them at risk of losing good stores when others shut their doors.

Figure 4-5

Consumer Confidence, Q1 2000 to Q1 2009
(Q1 1996 = 100)

Source: Reuters/University of Michigan.

The biggest sales hits are being felt at upscale apparel and home decor stores. Long-struggling Sears relies on sales of its appliances and home entertainment items; but with the weak housing market, consumers are buying only when their existing models no longer work and cannot be fixed. Wealthy American shoppers discovered Wal-Mart, Target, and off-price chains years ago (especially for children's items) and are shifting more of their spending—if they are spending at all—to these stores. Department store sales are hurting, despite a constant barrage of sales and coupon promotions. Consumers are "shopping down" and are not afraid to admit it. (A similar trend is seen in Japan, where young women's conspicuous spending on designer jewelry, shoes, and handbags is rapidly disappearing.)

The fierce competition between full-line and discount grocers seen in Europe is not as evident in the United States. Aldi is planning additional U.S. locations, where its competitors include Sav-A-Lot, Grocery Outlet, and smaller odd-lot local operators with colorful names (Cheap Charley's Surplus, Bent-N-Dent, and others). Nonetheless, discounters are said to attract less than 2 percent of America's grocery dollar.

Supermarkets were showing other signs of change before the economic downturn. Store sizes started to shrink for the first time in 20 years. Wal-Mart and Giant Eagle experimented with smaller formats focusing on fresh items and prepared meals. Drug chains such as CVS are stocking more food, snacks, paper goods, and cleaning products. Global grocery giant Tesco entered the United States, not with full-size supermarkets but with Fresh & Easy, a downsized format targeted to time-pressed working families. The planned rollout was quickly curtailed, perhaps because of disappointing performance but also as a result of the changing economic landscape.

ONLINE SHOPPING GROWS

U.S. retail sales (excluding automobiles, car parts, and gasoline) increased 41 percent between 2000 and 2008, but growth in catalog and e-commerce (up 91 percent) was much stronger.[13] Preliminary numbers for 2008 suggest that nonstore retailing accounted

VALERIE S. KRETSCHMER ASSOCIATES

Church Street Plaza, Evanston, Illinois.

New Ways to Shop: Beyond Online Sales

In a recent paper on changes in consumer demographics and shopping habits, Deloitte LLP observes:

> The marketplace is becoming far more transparent than it has ever been. In this new world order, nearly all individuals will likely have real-time access to information that previously was difficult or impossible to obtain. Increasingly, U.S. consumers will scan bar codes while in the store to see if they can buy it for less elsewhere. This is already the norm in Japan. Or they could band together on a Website, and once a critical mass is reached, they'll demand a 'bulk purchase' discount from a retailer. This 'mobshopping' phenomenon is picking up interest in China. . . . While Millennials (consumers in their twenties, mostly) are the driving force behind many of these trends, consumers of nearly all ages are quickly embracing the new technologies.

Increasingly savvy consumers are using the Internet to read product reviews from their peers (age specified), compare prices, share photos of favorites with their friends, and use social networking sites and YouTube to get the word out about what they like and do not like. With the many ways to find out about price, quality, and durability, consumers gain the upper hand in shopping decisions, and store or brand name loyalty declines.

Web retailers are becoming highly focused, offering new product lines that cater to niche consumers. As Deloitte points out, success can be fleeting, so both stores and online retailers should identify products that appeal to multiple groups of like-minded consumers. Items will need to be available on a variety of platforms—in stores, online, and through catalogs and call centers.

Source: Deloitte LLP, "The Changing Customer," Deloitte Retail Growth Challenge Framework Series #8, 2008.

for 7 percent of all sales not related to automobiles. Brick-and-mortar stores have successfully moved online but still capture less than half of nonstore trade. The balance is processed by Web-only retailers (such as Amazon.com), catalog sales and call centers, and brand manufacturers.

Traditional retailers are finding creative ways to sell merchandise online. To stimulate spending in a nervous market, online retailers are offering free shipping and discounts at least as good as those available for in-store purchases. College students (or their parents) can go to a local Bed Bath & Beyond or Target or use their Websites to order dorm room items online and pick them up at a store near the college—or have them delivered to the school.

Frugality: Everything Old Is New Again

In response to higher unemployment, wage cutbacks, sagging stock portfolios, and falling home values, middle-class households in Europe and Northern America are returning to old ways of being frugal:

▸▸ **CUTTING UP CREDIT CARDS**; using layaway programs to pay for purchases over time. During the 2008 holiday season, such American retailers as Kmart and Sears revived long-dormant layaway programs, allowing shoppers to pay a portion of the cost of their purchases each week and take them home only when the store has been fully paid. A small upfront fee is charged for the service. This works well for Christmas presents, but a household that needs winter coats or boots will not want to wait until February to claim them from the layaway office. An option for online shoppers: eLayaway.com's installment payment plans. Such plans are popular in Mexico, where retailers profit from interest charges.

▸▸ **PAYDAY LOANS.** Households are relying more on "cash advances"—long a staple of finance in poor neighborhoods with little access to conventional banks—to make ends meet.

▸▸ **EATING FEWER RESTAURANT MEALS**; packing a lunch to take to work. These trends are not good for the restaurant business.

▸▸ **MAKING FEWER VISITS TO THE GOURMET TAKEOUT COUNTER** or coffee shop. Coffee sales at Starbucks have plummeted, while McDonald's and Dunkin Donuts are selling more cups.

▸▸ **BUYING IN BULK AT WAREHOUSE CLUBS**, primarily for nonperishable items. This approach kept sales levels relatively healthy at Costco, BJ's, and Sam's Club in 2008. But it works only for those who have ample storage space or can share bulk purchases with family or friends.

▸▸ **SHOPPING FOR DISCOUNT GROCERIES** at stores that undercut prices offered by the competition. Wal-Mart Supercenter's groceries are benefiting from consumers' need to cut food bills, as are sales of supermarket chains' private labels.

▸▸ **BUYING APPAREL AND GIFTS AT OFF-PRICE RETAILERS.** Stores such as Marshalls, T. J. Maxx, and Ross Dress for Less offer name brands—even some designer goods—at terrific prices.

▸▸ **SELLING POSSESSIONS.** Households look to pawn shops, eBay, and craigslist to raise cash.

▸▸ **RIDING DISCOUNT BUS LINES BETWEEN MAJOR CITIES.** Greyhound has always been around, but new bus companies are capturing a bigger market share. After years of cutthroat competition—and safety concerns—the quality of service has improved. Passengers ride on double-decker buses with Wi-Fi from Washington to New York for only $30 round trip. Service has expanded on the West Coast, with buses from Los Angeles to Phoenix, San Francisco, and Las Vegas, and in the Southeast. Riding the bus is also gaining popularity in Japan, where savings over express train tickets can be substantial.

▸▸ **GETTING AN UNLIMITED MOVIE RENTAL SUBSCRIPTION** or watching free movies on cable. This is not a trend for teenagers, but not going out to a theater is certainly a way that empty nesters are saving on movie ticket prices.

▸▸ **REPAIRING CARS INSTEAD OF BUYING NEW ONES.** This will benefit auto supply stores. Bicycles may substitute for short trips.

▸▸ **INVITING FRIENDS OVER FOR ENTERTAINMENT.** People entertain by playing board games rather than going out for a night on the town.

▸▸ **CLIPPING COUPONS.** Whether from circulars or retailers' frequent shopper programs, coupons build customer loyalty by providing discounts or rebates not available to the general public.

In the developing world, many of these "new" trends are not new at all—they are the way families live every day.

Real Estate Implications

Retailers will continue to seek cross-border locations, looking for underserved and growing markets:

▸▸ For mid-price goods, they will consider countries that offer opportunities for critical mass, identifying places where they have already attracted online customers and shoppers who patronized their stores while traveling for business or pleasure.

▸▸ Emerging economies that are able to maintain positive GDP growth in today's difficult environment—even in the range of 1 to 2 percent—will be much more attractive to retailers that are experiencing stalling sales in their current markets. Key constraints will be the availability of the right type of real estate and government receptivity to foreign investment.

▸▸ Teenagers and young adults will remain a targeted demographic for specialty stores looking for new expansion outlets worldwide.

▸▸ The Internet will pose an ever-increasing challenge to traditional brick-and-mortar stores—and not only in the world's richer countries. Online sales will suffer during the recession, but the pain will be milder than that felt at mall shops.

▸▸ The credit crunch has made it impossible for developers in the United States, Canada, western Europe, and Japan to start new projects, even if they have an array of stable committed tenants.

▸▸ Owners with good properties in top locations will focus on retenanting any empty spaces and doing modest renovations to keep their centers attractive.

In the United States, the recession and the rise of Generation Y as consumers will shape the retail landscape:

▸▸ Successful chains will slow their expansion plans as customers battle unemployment and adopt more frugal buying habits.

▸▸ Discount grocers will capitalize on their recent sales surge by expanding to new metropolitan areas. They seek less expensive secondary locations and are unwilling to pay the rents associated with new, top-quality neighborhood and community shopping centers. Discounters may be willing to take over empty big-box spaces in the range of 20,000 to 25,000 square feet (the size of a former Linens 'n Things).

▸▸ Although Generation Y shoppers grew up at the mall, they will rebel against sameness. Seeing the same brands and the same designs throughout the mall is boring. Retailers have to attract these shoppers, because baby boomers and retirees do not need more "stuff." In a consumer survey sponsored by Wharton and the Verde Group, 35 percent of respondents—irrespective of age—complained about the lack of anything new or exciting at malls, and 28 percent mentioned that too many stores carried the same goods.[14]

▸▸ Customers will spread their dissatisfaction not only by word of mouth but in blogs and social networking sites; retailers must beware the customers who know more about products and pricing than the sales staff.

"Whatever economic doldrums retailers find themselves in, the reality is that economic growth will eventually return and surviving retailers will need to seek new arenas for expanding. Home markets for developed country retailers are going to be slow growing, saturated, and prone to excessive regulatory interference. To achieve rapid growth, successful retailers will be wise to seek out new territories. What better time to think about the dawn than when things are darkest?"

—Ira Kalish, *Revisiting Retail Globalization*, Deloitte Research, December 2008, p. 1

Milan, Italy.

Europe | 5

This year's edition of *Global Demographics* features three world regions: Europe, MENA, and sub-Saharan Africa (the latter two are presented in chapter 6). Europe has been a favored destination for American and Canadian real estate investors interested in geographic diversification. Retail chains based in Europe have spread to Canada and the United States, and Northern American specialty retailers and restaurants have long sought locations in Europe's growing supply of modern shopping centers.

Although Europe may seem familiar to American observers, its population and labor force characteristics are very different from those of Northern America. Demographically, the United States and Canada are more similar to Australia than to most European nations, with the exception of the United Kingdom:

▸▸ Europe's population is older.

▸▸ Although Europe had a baby boom after World War II, the size and influence of its "echo" boom are far less significant than in America.

▸▸ Fertility rates in every European country are below replacement levels.

▸▸ European workers retire earlier, on average, and a higher proportion of workers is covered by defined-benefit pension plans. Despite concerns about the viability of America's Social Security system when the large baby boom generation is fully retired, the number of working adults supporting children, retirees, and the disabled will be higher in the United States than in most of Europe.

▸▸ Average household sizes are smaller in Europe. Families typically have fewer children than in Northern America, but extended families living together are more common.

▸▸ Multifamily housing is the norm in Europe.

▸▸ Surprisingly, despite the age of its cities, Europe's population is less urbanized than Northern America's.

▸▸ In European metropolitan areas, low-income households tend to live in outlying suburbs; they are not concentrated in central cities.

Many European nations rely increasingly on immigrants to fill job vacancies, both skilled and unskilled. Europe's slowly shrinking workforce created job opportunities for immigrants from the Middle East, Africa, and South America during the recent economic boom. Expansion of the European Union also allowed young adults from former Soviet bloc countries to move freely to the West in search of better-paying jobs. In both Northern America and Europe, the addition of immigrant households spurred housing construction, contributed to inflated home prices and rents, and created opportunities for retail entrepreneurship. Remittances sent to family members improved lives—and economies—in emigrants' home countries. Now the tide is turning: the spreading recession has prompted many newcomers to return to their countries of origin,[1] and the number of in-migrants is shrinking as work options dry up. In addition, country after country is making it more difficult for low-wage workers without education or skills to cross borders in search of jobs.

Population Trends

As figure 1-2 showed in chapter 1, Europe's population is projected to decrease by 3.3 percent between 2007 and 2030—a reduction of nearly 24.3 million people in a period when growth will continue in all other regions of the world. In eastern Europe—the subregion with the most serious losses—a decline of more than 12 percent is anticipated.

Source: UN Population Division, *World Urbanization Prospects: The 2007 Revision*, tables A.1 and A.5.

Figure 5-1

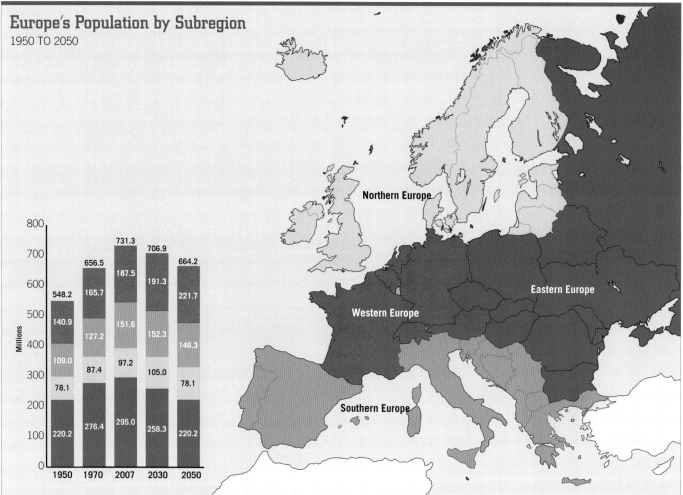

Figure 5-2

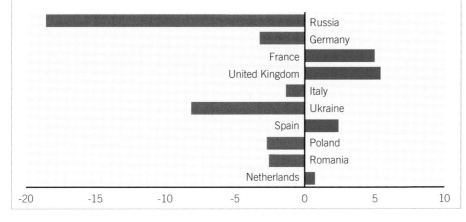

Population Change in Europe's Ten Biggest Countries
2007 TO 2030 (MILLIONS)

Source: UN Population Division, *World Urbanization Prospects: The 2007 Revision*, tables A.1 and A.5.

Going forward to 2050, only northern Europe will register small gains, attributable to immigration to the Scandinavian countries, the United Kingdom, and Ireland.

All four of Europe's subregions registered population gains between 1970 and 2007, as shown in figure 5-1, but regional aggregates tell only part of the story. Population decline in Europe is not a future phenomenon: it has been happening for more than two decades in Bulgaria and Hungary and since 1990 in Russia and Ukraine. In Germany, Spain, and the United Kingdom, losses experienced in the post–World War II era were reversed, largely by immigration. Fertility rates in Germany and southern Europe remain low.

Even though migration to prosperous countries is expected to resume after this recession, most European countries will be losing significant numbers of consumers by 2030 and beyond. Figure 5-2 lists Europe's ten largest countries, ranked by their 2007 population, and shows changes projected by UN demographers. Only four of the big ten European countries will grow; together, Russia and Ukraine will lose nearly 27 million consumers. Population loss is endemic across eastern Europe.

The diverse age characteristics of European nations are illustrated by the population pyramids in figure 5-3. In 1970, Ireland had relatively few adults age 25 to 44, as young workers moved overseas in search of better opportunities. In 2007, the country was attracting newcomers. Spain's population is rapidly aging, even though it is projected to grow by over 5 percent between 2007 and 2030. The shorter average life span for Russian men is reflected in the fact that men age 55 to 74 will account for only 8 percent of the country's total population in 2010, whereas women in this age group will constitute 12 percent.

European governments, eager to stem the tide of demographic decline, are creating incentives to raise birthrates:

➡ Municipalities are paying cash bonuses or prizes to families that have children. (Payments are staggered to ensure that the families remain in the community after a child is born.)

"Under communism, factories often provided free child care and higher salaries for parents with big families. But when communism collapsed, such policies disappeared. Combined with economic uncertainty, this sent postcommunist nations tumbling into uncharted territory, with fertility rates falling even more precipitously than they had in the Mediterranean. . . . It explains why fewer children were born at a particular time, but not why childbearing stayed low. After all, there is no obvious reason why parents should choose to have only one child just because the Berlin Wall has come down. Events with huge political significance may be, in demographic terms, just blips from which countries will recover sooner or later. It is still possible that will happen. Women who were 20 when the wall fell have not yet reached the end of their childbearing years. Perhaps birthrates will bounce back. But do not bet on it."

—"Suddenly, the Old World Looks Younger," *The Economist*, June 16, 2007, p. 29

- Nearly 70 percent of Russian pregnancies reportedly end in abortion; the country's abortion rate is 2.5 times that of western Europe.[2] Because contraceptives were difficult and costly to obtain under communist rule, Russians became accustomed to using abortion as birth control. Divorce rates are also high. To ramp up the birthrate, Russia declared 2008 the "Year of the Family" and held special events like the official "Day of Family, Love, and Fidelity." Billboards promoting family life are everywhere, and women who have a second or third child can receive a cash bonus.[3]

- Scandinavian countries have Europe's highest fertility rates because of the social support networks available to families with children. Norway provides 54 weeks of mater-

Figure 5-3a

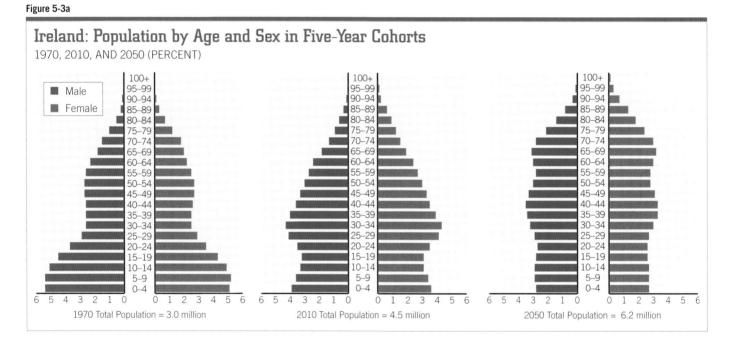

Ireland: Population by Age and Sex in Five-Year Cohorts
1970, 2010, AND 2050 (PERCENT)

1970 Total Population = 3.0 million   2010 Total Population = 4.5 million   2050 Total Population = 6.2 million

Figure 5-3b

Spain: Population by Age and Sex in Five-Year Cohorts
1970, 2010, AND 2050 (PERCENT)

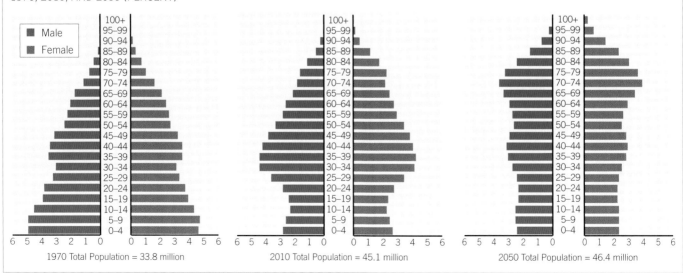

1970 Total Population = 33.8 million   2010 Total Population = 45.1 million   2050 Total Population = 46.4 million

Figure 5-3c

Russia: Population by Age and Sex in Five-Year Cohorts
1970, 2010, AND 2050 (PERCENT)

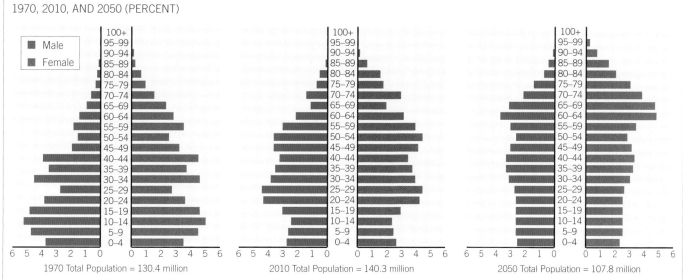

1970 Total Population = 130.4 million

2010 Total Population = 140.3 million

2050 Total Population = 107.8 million

Source Figure 5a, 5b, 5c: *UN Population Division, World Population Prospects: The 2006 Revision*, http://esa.un.org/unpp.

nity leave (at 80 percent salary), with six weeks off for new fathers. The government provides a cash payment of about €4,000 and offers state-subsidized daycare for working parents.

▸▸ In contrast, Italy provides little in the way of government assistance for families with children. As is the case in the United States, it is more difficult to rely on parents and grandparents for child care because extended families are increasingly dispersed.[4] Childbearing out of wedlock is frowned upon and, with limited career opportunities for young adults, marriage and childbearing are delayed. Over 70 percent of Italians under age 30 live at home with their parents.[5]

▸▸ French mothers get a minimum of 16 weeks of paid leave, increasing to 26 weeks at the birth of a third child. Prekindergarten is free, and care for younger babies is subsidized. A woman who has a third child gets the equivalent of $960 per month for a year (twice the allowance for a second child); the government provides other cash allowances—including funds to pay for extracurricular arts and sports activities—and tax incentives.[6]

▸▸ In the United Kingdom, working mothers get six months of paid leave (with an option for another six months of unpaid absence) and fathers get two weeks. Four-year-olds can attend part-time preschool programs free of charge. The United Kingdom has one of Europe's highest fertility rates.

▸▸ Germany covers two-thirds of a new parent's salary (up to €1,800 per month) for a year and is embarking on a program to build more daycare centers. (Leaving young children in all-day nurseries used to be socially unacceptable; kindergartens end their day at 1 p.m., creating strains for working parents.) Germany's 2006 crude birthrate was only eight per 1,000 people, well below that of France (13), the United Kingdom (13), Russia (12), and Spain (11).[7]

Figure 5-4

Change in Fertility Rates, Selected European Countries

(NUMBER OF BIRTHS PER WOMAN)

	1996	2006
Eastern Europe		
Bulgaria	1.23	1.38
Poland	1.53	1.28
Russia	1.27	1.31
Ukraine	1.33	1.25
Northern Europe		
Ireland	1.89	1.90
Latvia	1.18	1.35
Norway	1.89	1.90
Sweden	1.61	1.85
Southern Europe		
Croatia	1.64	1.38
Greece	1.28	1.40
Italy	1.20	1.35
Spain	1.16	1.37
Western Europe		
Austria	1.45	1.41
France	1.73	1.98
Germany	1.32	1.40
Netherlands	1.53	1.73

Source: Population Reference
Bureau, 2007, http://www.prb.org.

Figure 5-5

European Urban Areas by Size and Projected Growth Rate
2006 TO 2020

ESTIMATED 2006 POPULATION

1 to 1.5 Million	1.5 to 5 Million	5 Million Plus
Amsterdam	Athens	Moscow
Dublin	Lisbon	Dortmund-Bochum (Ruhr)
Lille	Stockholm	London
Lyon	Barcelona	Madrid
Marseilles–Aix-en-Provence	Berlin	Paris
Newcastle-Gateshead	Brussels	Saint Petersburg
Porto	Cologne-Bonn	
Rotterdam	Dusseldorf-Essen	
Zurich	Frankfurt-Wiesbaden	
Aachen	Hamburg	
Bielefeld	Kiev	
Copenhagen	Lisbon	
Dnipropetrovsk	Madrid	
Glasgow	Mannheim-Heidelberg	
Hamburg	Minsk	
Hannover	Munich	
Munich	Stuttgart	
Nurnberg	Warsaw	
Sofia	Vienna	
Belgrade	Birmingham	
Chelyabinsk	Bucharest	
Ekaterinburg	Budapest	
Kazan	Katowice	
Kharkov	Manchester	
Leeds	Milan	
Nizhniy Novgorod	Naples	
Novosibirsk	Rome	
Omsk		
Prague		
Rostov-on-Don		
Samara		
Turin		
Ufa		

Change from 2006 to 2020
Average Annual Growth Rate of 0.3 Percent or More
Stable: Average Annual Growth of Less Than 0.3 Percent
Decline

Source: http://www.citymayors.com.

Evidence that fertility rates are rising in some European countries can be seen in figure 5-4. No countries have returned to replacement levels (2.1 children per woman), but some are close: the French vital statistics agency indicates that the country's 2008 fertility level was just over 2.0 and claims that it has the highest rate in Europe at present. (Ireland is second.) Over 800,000 babies were born in France in 2008, the highest for a single year in three decades.[8] Births rose by more than 5 percent between 2004 and 2006 in the Czech Republic, Bulgaria, Sweden, and Hungary.[9]

What is not clear from national statistics is the extent to which the recent rise in fertility can be attributed to government incentives, a changing attitude toward childbearing, the higher age at which women are first giving birth, or in-migration of young women from countries where large families are the norm. For example, birthrates are higher among Muslim women compared with native residents. Although the French government does not collect birth statistics by religion, one study found that immigrant women had a fertility rate of 2.5 compared with 1.65 for French-born women.[10] Some observers suggest that Europe could have a majority-Muslim population by 2100. It will be interesting to see how the current recession affects fertility rates, because immigration is likely to drop and fiscally strapped governments will be hard pressed to continue generous profamily incentives.

Urban Growth and Decline

Moscow is the only global megacity—an urban agglomeration with more than 10 million people—located in Europe; but by 2025, urbanized Paris will squeeze into this category. London is the only other European metropolitan area with over 5 million people. (Istanbul is discussed in chapter 6.)

Most urban areas on the continent are growing very slowly if at all. Figure 5-5 lists Europe's 66 urbanized areas with populations of 1 million or more, of which only 12 are projected to register growth of more than 0.3 percent annually from 2006 to 2020.

Limited regional population growth curtails demand for housing and retail space, even when the need to replace obsolete or deteriorated buildings is taken into account. And as urban areas spread and consume more agricultural and forest land, empty or marginal structures are left behind. In downtown cores, where demand has traditionally been strong, publicly or privately funded redevelopment efforts create new competitive product. In inner-ring suburbs—especially those that lack good transit access—demand may be weak and aggressive demolition programs will be needed to keep markets in balance.

Although metropolitan London has fewer people than Moscow or Paris, it is Europe's dominant financial center and has challenged New York for global preeminence. Despite years of worrying about competition from Frankfurt and Brussels, London firms were handling 70 percent of global international bonds, one-third of currency trading, and almost half the volume of global equity trading in 2008. Financial activities accounted for nearly 20 percent of London's economy, compared with 15 percent in New York City.[12] As international banking and investment companies located their European headquarters in London, new upscale housing—and escalating rents and prices for older units—soon followed.

The current financial crisis will hurt London more than other European cities with diversified economies. London's redevelopment and construction of new office space exceeded that in Paris, which has been more concerned about preserving and renovating historic buildings. Even though occupancy will suffer, demographics favor London. Immigration has caused London's population to surge, while Paris's core is projected to lose people as its suburbs spread out. Also, London's immigrants are better educated than those in Paris.[13]

Working in Europe

With Europe's economic expansion during the mid-2000s, unemployment fell sharply. The drop was most dramatic in eastern European and Baltic states, perhaps because of young workers' migration to the West. The global economic crisis caused this five-year trend to reverse in 2008; by November, overall EU unemployment had risen to 7.2 percent from 6.9 percent a year earlier, and youth unemployment climbed by 1.7 percentage points.

A Shrinking Russian City

Ivanovo, located 300 kilometers northeast of Moscow, had 431,721 inhabitants during the 2002 Russian Census; by 2006, its population was estimated to have shrunk to just over 413,000. The census population count for the Ivanovo *oblast* (province) was 1,148,329; it was estimated to have dropped to just under 1.1 million at the start of 2006.

Architect Philip Oswalt, with the Shrinking Cities project, suggests the reasons for Ivanovo's losses: "Beginning in the mid-nineteenth century, the region developed into the center of the Russian textile industry. . . . The demise of the Soviet Union plunged the city into an unprecedented economic crisis. Uzbekistan stopped sending cotton. Sales shrank as a result of sudden competition from western Europe and the Far East. Industrial production dropped by around 80 percent. Both the birthrate and life expectancy declined dramatically. It is above all the younger, better-educated people who leave Ivanovo in search of work. Yet in spite of the drastic economic situation, population loss has remained moderate because mobility is limited."

Source: http://www.citypopulation.de; Philipp Oswalt, "Shrinking Cities," in *Complete Works 3: Case Study: Japan*, chapter 1, p. 5, www.shrinkingcities.com.

Figure 5-6

Employment of Persons Age 55 to 64, as a Share of All Persons That Age

(PERCENT)

	1997	2002	2007
EU-27	**36.2**	**38.5**	**44.7**
Selected Countries			
Bulgaria	—	27.0	42.6
Czech Republic	—	40.8	46.0
France	29.0	34.7	38.3
Germany	38.1	38.9	51.5
Greece	41.0	39.2	42.4
Hungary	17.7	25.6	33.1
Ireland	40.4	48.0	53.8
Italy	27.9	28.9	33.8
Lithuania	—	41.6	53.4
Poland	33.9	26.1	29.7
Romania	52.1	37.3	41.4
Spain	34.1	39.6	44.6
Sweden	62.6	68.0	70.0
United Kingdom	48.3	53.4	57.4
United States	57.1	59.4	61.8
Japan	64.2	61.6	66.1

— = not available.
Note: EU-27 = all members of the European Union.

Source: Eurostat. http://epp.eurostat.ec.europa.eu.

Figure 5-7

Projected Old-Age Dependency Ratios

(PERSONS AGE 65 AND OLDER AS A PERCENTAGE OF THE WORKING-AGE POPULATION)

	2010	2030	2050
EU-27	**26**	**38**	**51**
Selected Countries			
Czech Republic	22	36	55
France	26	39	45
Germany	31	46	56
Greece	28	38	57
Hungary	24	34	51
Ireland	17	25	40
Italy	31	42	59
Lithuania	23	35	51
Netherlands	23	40	46
Norway	23	34	41
Poland	19	36	56
Slovakia	17	32	56
Spain	24	34	59
Sweden	28	37	42
Switzerland	25	38	46
United Kingdom	25	33	38

Note: EU-27 = all members of the European Union.

Source: Eurostat. http://epp.eurostat.ec.europa.eu.

When the electorate faces job losses, governments focus on stimulating job creation, not expanding the workforce; however, in the long run, Europe needs to look at how it will provide the labor necessary for future growth.

For office developers and investors, trends in the labor force are more important than population growth in predicting future demand. Europe's working-age population (age 15 to 64) will decline faster than its total residents. As seen in appendix 2, a drop in the percentage of working-age people is anticipated in every European country between 2005 and 2030. In nations where the birthrate has held up and immigration has augmented the young adult population (such as Ireland and the United Kingdom), the decline will be relatively small. This is also true in a number of former Soviet bloc countries that have not yet experienced significant gains in longevity.

Contraction of the working-age population is troubling because rising dependency ratios (the number of children or retirees per 1,000 workers) strain social support systems, creating fiscal problems for national and local governments. A shortage of workers—especially for skilled positions—raises wages and deters investment by companies that want to expand. It also creates pressure to bring in immigrant labor, a situation that is then difficult to reverse when economies decelerate.

Europe's recent and future labor shortages stem not only from low fertility rates and shrinking numbers of working-age persons. A glaring issue highlighted in chapter 2 is the relative absence of older European adults in the labor force. As figure 5-6 shows, 2007 labor force participation rates for persons age 55 to 64 are quite low compared with those of the United States and Japan. Sweden is the only country where more than 70 percent of people in this age group are working (even part-time) or actively seeking employment. Nonetheless, recent increases in Germany and Lithuania are impressive.

One reason for low employment among older adults is the early retirement ages common in Europe. Residents of Croatia, France, Poland, and the Slovak Republic typically retire (with full benefits) before age 60, and those in Belgium, the Czech Republic, Finland, and Italy do so before age 62. Italy has the lowest employment ratio for older adults of all the countries shown in figure 5-6; only a third of its population age 55 to 64 was employed. Making matters worse, some countries have offered generous early retirement programs or pay higher unemployment benefits to workers age 50 or older, thereby discouraging them from returning to the workforce.

Of great concern is the increasing old-age dependency ratio throughout Europe—the number of persons age 65 and older relative to the working-age population. Eurostat projections presented in figure 5-7 suggest that the incidence of old-age dependency will nearly double in the 27 nations that are part of the European Union. By 2050, there will be fewer than two working-age adults supporting every senior citizen, compared with nearly four in 2010. Italy and Spain will have the highest dependency ratios among the countries shown in the chart; the United Kingdom, Norway, and Ireland will have the lowest. Although Russia's dependency ratio is not shown,[14] it is deceptively low because Russia's life expectancy, especially for men, is well below European averages—attributable to poor health care services, a high incidence of alcoholism, inadequate sleep, and what some observers have called "nicotine genocide."[15] Higher dependency ratios cause pension and senior service costs to escalate, with fewer taxpaying workers to fund them. European governments already spend a high share of GDP on pensions.

The good news is that tightening labor markets are pushing change. As was reflected in figure 5-6, the percentage of people age 55 to 64 who were working increased between 1997 and 2007 in all countries shown except Greece, Poland, and Romania. (Definitional changes over time may explain some of these anomalies.) Significant gains were also recorded in Germany, Ireland, and the United Kingdom. Liberal retirement and pension programs are gradually being revised to reflect demographic realities:

▸▸ Italy has slowly increased its retirement age to 59.

▸▸ French government employees must work for 40 years before reaching full pension eligibility. President Sarkozy wants to extend this requirement to the entire workforce, though the formal retirement age would still be 60.

▸▸ Germany raised its retirement age by two years, to 67. However, efforts to curtail growth in public pension obligations have met resistance. Reportedly, 11 million Germans now have private pension plans.[16]

▸▸ Individually directed private retirement savings plans have been established in the Baltic states, Bulgaria, Poland, Romania, and Sweden.

▸▸ The Czech Republic's parliament has passed a bill that would increase the retirement age to 65 by 2030.

Not surprisingly, such changes encounter resistance from older residents, but public opinion polls suggest widespread recognition of the need for action. Meanwhile, labor force participation rates for young adults have been rising, even though more are pursuing tertiary education. Women have already been integrated into Europe's workforce, and although their labor force participation still lags that of men, it is unlikely that many additional workers can be squeezed from the ranks of young women. Ethnic and religious differences in attitudes toward education of women, their participation in the workplace, and home responsibilities limit that potential source of skilled employees.

Coping with Migration

The presence of racial and ethnic minorities in Europe is not new. As a consequence of colonial attachments, language ties, and guest worker programs, immigrant enclaves have been commonplace in Europe's large cities; however, during the recent economic expansion, western, southern, and northern Europe attracted immigrants from eastern Europe, as well as from traditional sources in Africa, the Middle East, and South America. Figure 5-8 lists the European nations with the largest numbers of foreigners residing within their borders as of 2007. Germany had nearly twice the number as the United Kingdom and France. Switzerland, Belgium, and Austria—three relatively small countries—are also in the top ten. As discussed in last year's *Global Demographics*, Austria has been the gateway for trade between western Europe and the former Soviet bloc. Switzerland and Belgium

"Early retirement among EU workers, and in particular, the fact that 55 percent of 55- to 64-year-olds are not contributing to the European economy, is playing a key part in weakening the sustainability of European pension systems. . . . A positive sign that this issue is being addressed is shown by the increase in the average retirement age across Europe in the past year from 60.5 to 61 years. . . . To cope with demographic changes and challenges to economies, pension reforms continue to be popular across Europe, with the trend being to cut back in state schemes. . . . In Europe, the countries with the worst problems tend to be those where the average retirement age is low and they face major demographic and social security issues, which, if not addressed, will create unsustainable pension systems. The rising pressure an ageing population is placing on government expenditure can be mitigated by government encouraging greater use of funded pensions, which mean that today's workers pay for their own pensions instead of relying on the next generation to do so."

—Aon Consultings (London), "Early Retirement Weakening European Pension Systems," *European Pensions Barometer*, 13 November 2007.

Figure 5-8

European Countries with the Largest Number of Foreign Residents

2007

	Number	Share of Population (Percent)
Germany	7,255,949	9
Spain	4,606,474	10
United Kingdom	3,659,900	6
France	3,650,100	6
Italy	2,938,922	5
Switzerland	1,554,527	21
Belgium	932,161	11
Greece	887,600	8
Austria	826,013	10
Netherlands	681,932	4

Source: Eurostat, http://epp.eurostat.ec.europa.eu.

(the capital of the European Union) have large corps of diplomats, financial executives, and other professionals from all over the world.

Within the EU nations, labor movement is fluid. As additional former Soviet bloc countries gained admission to the European Union, their young, educated labor forces sought well-paying technology jobs in the West. Travel was not restricted, and work permits were not always needed (though only Ireland, the United Kingdom, and Sweden fully opened their borders to countries that joined the European Union after 2004). In an era of global economic expansion, the rising tide lifted all boats and eastern and central European countries prospered despite their loss of young workers. In western and northern Europe as well as in Spain, jobs in construction, restaurants, and households were plentiful for newcomers who lacked skills. Remittances sent home by immigrants, both legal and illegal, boosted purchasing power worldwide.

As the global economy turned down in 2008, public attitudes toward immigration (tolerant, if not supportive, during the boom years) took a new direction. Increasing hostility toward immigrants is directed particularly at the growing Muslim population, but others (such as ethnic Romas, or gypsies) have also felt the anger.

SPAIN

More than 800,000 in-migrants arrived in Spain in 2006 alone. Its foreign population rose to 10 percent by early 2007, and the percentage of foreign workers in the labor force rose from 8 percent in 2005 to 12 percent two years later. In 2005, 560,000 immigrants from northern Africa and Latin America were legalized, along with their family members.[17] A recent *New York Times* article summarized how quickly things changed:

> Spain created more jobs and drew more immigrants than any other country in Europe in the past decade, largely because of a construction boom. As the economy shrinks, employers are disgorging workers quickly—unemployment soared to more than 11 percent in the third quarter [of 2008]—and immigrants in low-skilled jobs have been hit the hardest. The once permissive Spanish government is rolling up the welcome mat, even encouraging immigrants to return home in exchange for lump-sum welfare payments (and agreement not to return for three years). Spain has not yet suffered the xenophobia heard in places like Italy, and Spaniards say their own years as a nation of émigrés help them sympathize.... But hospitality may wear thin. Spain's unemployment rate (at 13.9 percent in December 2008) is now the highest in the European Union, up from 8 percent at the end of 2007. Among immigrants, unemployment is estimated at 17 percent. About five million immigrants are registered as living in Spain, a country of 46 million, with Moroccans, Romanians, and Ecuadoreans topping the list.[18]

Thousands of immigrants do not qualify for unemployment benefits because they worked illegally or without formal contracts. The authorities are enforcing employment laws and checking papers. (The European Union now permits illegal immigrants to be detained for up to 18 months pending deportation.) Foreign agricultural workers are being replaced by locals, and farmers are giving jobs to needy relatives. Immigrants who once worked in

the construction industries are sitting idle, along with Spanish nationals who were very busy during the housing boom. Even so, most immigrants are determined to stay, especially if one spouse is still working or the family includes school-age children. Only 1,400 foreigners took advantage of the government's cash-payment offer to exit during the first two months of its availability.[19]

THE UNITED KINGDOM

The United Kingdom granted immediate labor market access to countries admitted to the European Union in 2004, effectively legalizing hundreds of thousands of eastern Europeans already working there and allowing many more to enter. Polish nationals quickly became the largest contemporary immigrant group, growing from about 53,000 in early 2004 to 447,000 by the end of 2007. With the rise in unemployment rates, many are returning home; and at the same time, the United Kingdom is tightening the number of work visas it issues, even for skilled occupations.[20]

ITALY

Approximately 3 million foreign nationals resided legally in Italy in 2007 (5 percent of the population); illegal immigrants added an additional 670,000. Anti-immigrant sentiment is on the rise, targeted toward Romanians and Africans. As EU members, Romanian citizens can live legally in Italy without special permits, whereas workers from non-EU countries must demonstrate that they have a job and housing in order to work legally.[21]

GERMANY

In recent years, Poland has sourced more immigration to Germany than any other country. However, Turks are Germany's largest ethnic minority, having migrated in search of work for nearly 50 years. Despite a law passed in 2000 that permitted nonethnic Germans to be naturalized, two-thirds of the country's 2.6 million Turkish residents are not German citizens. Ethnic Turks account for 29 percent of the unemployed, and their unemployment rate is double that of Germany as a whole. Efforts to prompt Turks to return home in the 1970s and 1980s were not successful; more often than not, guest workers eventually brought their families to Germany. Long important to Germany's heavy industries and supplementing its aging indigenous labor force, the Turkish minority was never well integrated into the nation's social fabric. The younger generation is better educated than their parents, and stronger efforts are being made to teach German to children as well as older adults. Even so, the school system is not fully successful in bringing young ethnic Turks—many of whom were born in Germany—into the mainstream.[22]

IRELAND

Irish in-migration came primarily from the eastern European countries in the European Union (Poland, Lithuania, and the Slovak Republic were the top three countries of origin) and from Nigeria. Now, with job opportunities in Ireland and the United Kingdom contracting, many European migrants are leaving, aided by Internet job sites that make them aware of attractive opportunities at home and by the widespread availability of discount airfares. Wage gaps are narrowing, and home countries will be able to use skilled help. The Polish government has an active campaign to encourage its citizens to return, bringing with them the money saved while working in the West.

The Nigerians are not so fortunate. Many are in the country illegally because a one-time legalization effort in 2005 was not extended. Consequently, Ireland has thousands of families with mixed citizenship, consisting of one or both parents residing illegally with their Irish-born children. (Children born in Europe to illegal immigrant parents are not automatically granted citizenship.) In Europe, as in the United States, efforts to deport illegal immigrants during an economic downturn can be politically popular, even though they may come at the expense of family cohesion.

FRANCE

Much has been written about France and its largely Muslim minorities who are concentrated at the outskirts of Paris and other large cities, often in cramped high-rise buildings that resemble the vilified public housing that is common in American inner cities (but gradually being demolished). Job opportunities for young Muslims in France have been more limited than for immigrants to Spain or Ireland, and political representation is only now emerging.

Until 2008, each EU member maintained its own immigration policies. To cope with the current economic downturn, EU nations are standardizing their rules, focusing on admitting mainly skilled workers for occupations that are still experiencing labor shortages. Border controls are being tightened.

Diversity in Marseilles

Multiethnic Marseilles, France's second largest city, is also its most diverse. Among its approximately 839,000 residents are 200,000 Muslims, 80,000 Orthodox Armenians, nearly 80,000 Jews, and 3,000 Buddhists. It houses 70,000 Comorans, second only to the number in Moroni, the capital of Comoros, in East Africa. Marseilles is a historic port city and visitor destination, attracting nearly a half million cruise passengers alone and providing the traditional gateway for immigrants from former French colonies.

Source: Andrew Purvis, "Marseille's Ethnic Bouillabaisse," *Smithsonian*, December 2007, p. 86.

Figure 5-9

Source: OECD, *OECD Factbook 2008.*

Educational Attainment of Recent Immigrants and Young Natives

2005 (PERCENT)

	FOREIGN-BORN LABOR FORCE*			NATIVE-BORN LABOR FORCE**		
	Low	Intermediate	High	Low	Intermediate	High
Austria	25.5	51.4	23.1	7.3	71.2	21.5
Belgium	32.2	24.9	42.9	14.9	41.6	43.5
France	40.7	25.6	33.7	15.9	43.1	41.0
Germany	32.7	41.0	26.3	9.8	64.9	25.3
Ireland	14.6	37.7	47.7	15.7	42.2	42.1
Italy	45.5	43.6	10.8	30.6	52.7	16.7
Netherlands	25.9	45.4	28.7	14.7	46.1	39.2
Spain	42.3	35.9	21.8	33.5	22.2	44.4
Sweden	21.4	40.3	38.3	7.1	54.6	38.4
Switzerland	23.9	33.9	42.2	2.4	64.5	33.2
United States	34.1	35.1	30.8	6.5	49.3	44.2

*Immigrants present in the country for no more than ten years. **Natives age 25 to 34.
Note: Low = did not complete upper secondary school; Intermediate = completed upper secondary school; High = completed tertiary education, which could include advanced vocational training.

Educational Attainment

European nations have attracted both highly educated and unskilled workers from beyond their borders. In some countries, recent newcomers are more educated than the native-born labor force; but in other nations, the reverse is true. Figure 5-9 compares the educational attainment of young, native-born residents and recent immigrants in the ten countries with the most foreigners. The United States is also shown for comparison.

According to the OECD, immigrants show lower levels of tertiary attainment than younger (age 25 to 34) native-born recent entrants to the labor force. When looking at the entire native-born labor force, irrespective of age, the education of immigrants compares favorably in some countries but not in others. For example, young native-born adults in France and the Netherlands are better educated than recent immigrants. In Switzerland and Ireland, the opposite is true.[23]

"High" educational attainment can include anything from completion of postsecondary vocational training to a doctoral or other advanced degree. What is clear from figure 5-9 is that the young, native-born labor force is more likely to have completed the equivalent of high school or beyond, but advanced education and training is widespread among newcomers to Belgium, Ireland, Switzerland, and Sweden. Contrast this with Italy, where both the foreign- and native-born labor forces have completed fewer years of school.

Households and Home Prices

Several European countries are suffering from the same collapse of housing prices experienced in the United States since 2007—and for much the same reasons:

▸▸ Demand was propelled by immigration-driven population growth.

▸▸ Young people with good jobs formed their own households rather than remain in their parents' homes.

- Mortgage money was plentiful and underwriting standards were eased to allow people with marginal credit histories to borrow. (In Spain, some say it was easier to get a mortgage than to rent an apartment.) When credit dried up, transaction volumes crashed.

- Rising prices, combined with interest rate hikes in 2007, put homebuying out of reach for more and more segments of demand.

- Consumers grew fearful as unemployment spiked quickly in 2008.

- Property owners—especially those who bought at or near the peak in prices—could no longer meet their obligations. Delinquency and repossession rates rose.

- Developers speculated in second-home developments (especially in sunny Spain, but also in Croatia and Portugal), catering to an increasingly affluent populace with a growing appetite for travel.

- Industrial cities (in the northern part of the United Kingdom, former East Germany, Russia, and Italy) are losing population and therefore have softer housing demand, similar to that seen in such American industrial cities as Detroit, Cleveland, Dayton, Buffalo, and Youngstown.

The Royal Institution of Chartered Surveyors predicts that home prices in the United Kingdom will fall by 25 percent from peak to trough, and 10 to 15 percent in 2009, before inching upward again, despite the fact that transaction volumes should pick up this year.[24] They caution that house prices and monthly mortgage payments are still high relative to household income. In contrast, home prices in Germany are stable because new supply has been on the decline for more than a decade. Poland's housing market held up well through 2008.

Not surprisingly, countries where population growth was steadiest—Spain, the United Kingdom, Ireland, the Netherlands, and France—have showed the highest price escalation. The average homeownership rate in those countries is roughly equal to the United States, but there is wide variation—from 82 percent of Spanish households to just 54 percent in the United Kingdom. Housing construction levels in Spain, Ireland, and Austria were well above the norm; however, Austria did not develop a price bubble and the other two did.

German townhouse from the 1930s.

Europe's many diverse housing markets have unique attributes not shared with America or Canada. Throughout the continent, housing in dense, historic urban cores is centuries old, and very difficult and costly to renovate. The shortage of new units drove up prices. In former communist countries, the shift to market-driven economies left unfilled voids. The private sector saw opportunity in upscale product that caters to increasingly affluent middle and upper classes, with little attention given to recent immigrants, poor families, or low-income seniors. (The stock of post–World War II housing is bleak and poorly constructed.)

Real Estate Implications

Do demographics equal destiny? Imminent population and labor force declines portend shrinking demand for real estate, suggesting that development opportunities will be limited to replacement of obsolete housing and retail space and that there will be less need for additions to the office inventory. It is important to remember, however, that population losses are not uniform across Europe and that factors used in mid-century population projections can certainly shift as 2030 or 2050 draws near:

▸ The United Kingdom, the Scandinavian countries, Ireland, and the Netherlands will continue to grow.

▸ Birthrates began rising again in Poland in 2003 after two decades of decline.

▸ Countries may tighten immigration policies as a short-term response to the recession, but most will, of necessity, open their borders again once economic conditions improve.

▸ As immigrants return to their home countries and as unemployment hampers new household formation, house prices will continue the slide that began in 2008. Hardest hit are Ireland, Spain, and the United Kingdom. Economic conditions in Germany have been more stable, with fewer peaks and valleys.

▸ Redevelopment and modernization of housing and retail space makes sense, but supply will need to be more closely monitored to match demand shifts.

▸ Changing space standards—for office workers and housing consumers—will support new construction, but demolition should accompany creation.

▸ Increasing affluence—especially in eastern Europe—will partially compensate for the smaller number of consumers.

▸ European governments recognize the need to modify their retirement policies, encouraging—and mandating—older workers to stay in the labor force.

▸ Urbanization and migration within countries will also generate demand. Some cities will continue to thrive, with vibrant office, retail, and entertainment cores. Others will contract.

Overall, however, Europe's need will be for replacement buildings, so demolition of older properties will need to match the volumes of new construction. Without net new demand, there cannot be net new supply, or vacancy will rise, rents will fall, and values will decline—not a pretty vision.

Tunis, Tunisia.

Middle East & Africa | 6

Two distinct subregions constitute this part of the world: the Middle East[1] and North Africa (MENA), which accounts for one-third of the population, as reflected in figure 6-1, and sub-Saharan Africa, which is the globe's fastest-growing area. From 2007 to 2030, an estimated 645 million people will be added to this overall region—growth of well over 50 percent. In the subsequent 20 years, another 540 million are projected, an additional 30 percent increase. Asia will actually have larger numerical growth in the earlier period but, as lower birthrates kick in between 2030 to 2050, Asia will add only half as many people as Africa and the Middle East. In this part

Figure 6-1

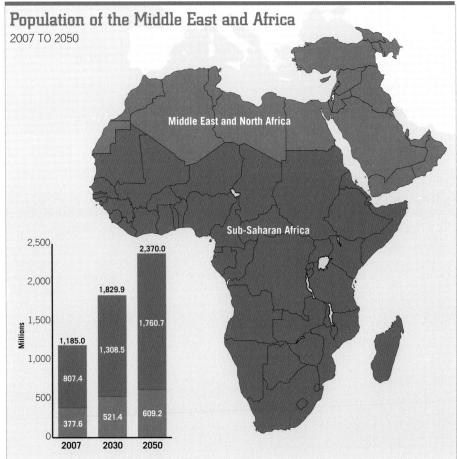

Population of the Middle East and Africa
2007 TO 2050

Middle East and North Africa

Sub-Saharan Africa

Source: UN Population Division, *World Urbanization Prospects: The 2007 Revision*, tables A.1 and A.5, http://esa.un.org/unup.

Gains by Algerian Women

"In this tradition-bound nation, . . . a quiet revolution is underway: women are emerging as an economic and political force unheard of in the rest of the Arab world.

▸▸ Women make up 70 percent of Algeria's lawyers and 60 percent of its judges.

▸▸ Women dominate medicine.

▸▸ Increasingly, women contribute more to household income than men.

▸▸ Sixty percent of university students are women."

Source: Michael Slackman, "A Quiet Revolution in Algeria," *The New York Times*, May 26, 2007, p. 1.

Oil: Sub-Saharan Africa's Number-One Commodity

African Business reports: "Since 2000, one-third of the world's new oil discoveries have taken place in [sub-Saharan] Africa. . . . From 2005 to 2010, 20 percent of the world's new production capacity is expected to come from Africa. . . . Despite this, Africa has only 10 percent of global oil reserves and is unlikely to replace the Middle Eastern oil supply." Nonetheless, most West African oil is high quality, with low sulfur content, so it is easily refined. Eight sub-Saharan countries are currently blessed with oil. Angola is the largest producer, followed by Nigeria and Sudan. The newest entrants to the industry are Ghana and Uganda.

Source: Emanuel Misghinna, "Can Africa Calm Market Fears?" *African Business*, August/September 2008, pp. 24–25.

of the world, sub-Saharan Africa will expand fastest—rising from two-thirds of the total to three-quarters by 2050.

The area encompasses 73 nations—23 in MENA and 50 in sub-Saharan Africa. Of the ten largest countries listed in figure 6-2, three are in MENA—Egypt, Turkey, and Algeria; by 2030, Uganda will join the group, displacing Algeria. South Africa will drop from sixth to tenth over the next 20 years. Truly startling growth is expected in the biggest sub-Saharan nations:

▸▸ 53 percent in Nigeria,

▸▸ 65 percent in Ethiopia, and

▸▸ 96 percent—virtual doubling—in the Democratic Republic of Congo.

This region's socioeconomic challenge in the first half of the 21st century is to improve the education and training of its abundant young population and then create enough meaningful jobs to put that population to work. While the world's working-age population will expand by 30 percent between 2005 and 2030, the size of the potential labor force will expand by 52 percent in MENA and 91 percent in sub-Saharan Africa. Generating employment on this scale will be daunting, requiring something akin to China's manufacturing miracle—on steroids and across 73 diverse political jurisdictions.

As discussed in chapter 2, working women contribute in two key ways to economic growth: by expanding a nation's productive workforce and by contributing to household income. This region displays a fascinating dichotomy: it contains most of the places in which few women work (below 30 percent), and it also contains the bulk of the nations in which the highest proportions of adult females are employed (over 70 percent). As illustrated in figure 6-3, the very low female employment-to-population ratios are predominantly in Muslim countries within the MENA subregion. Especially notable are Palestine, Iraq, Egypt, and Saudi Arabia.

In contrast, nine of the 11 countries with female labor force participation above 70 percent are in sub-Saharan Africa. Tanzania and Burundi, which report female participation of more than 80 percent, stand out as the two highest in the world. The majority of these African women are doing manual labor on small subsistence farms. On average, as will be discussed later in

Figure 6-2

Ten Largest Countries in MENA and Sub-Saharan Africa
2007 AND 2030 (MILLIONS)

Country	2007 Population	Rank	Country	2030 Population
Nigeria	148.1	1	Nigeria	226.9
Ethiopia	83.1	2	Ethiopia	137.1
Egypt	75.5	3	Democratic Republic of Congo	122.7
Turkey	75.5	4	Egypt	104.1
Democratic Republic of Congo	62.7	5	Turkey	92.5
South Africa	48.6	6	Tanzania	65.5
Tanzania	40.5	7	Kenya	62.7
Sudan	38.6	8	Uganda	61.5
Kenya	37.5	9	Sudan	58.4
Algeria	33.9	10	South Africa	53.2

Source: UN Population Division, *World Urbanization Prospects: The 2007 Revision*, tables A.1. and A.5. http://esa.un.org/unup.

this chapter, agriculture still accounts for a great deal of sub-Saharan employment, but in the MENA subregion it has become less important than industry and services.

MENA and sub-Saharan Africa vary in other important ways, as highlighted in figure 6-4. For instance, MENA's fertility rate of 2.9 children per woman, though well above replacement level, is far below sub-Saharan Africa's rate of 5.2. More than nine of ten young people in MENA finish primary school, whereas the figure in sub-Saharan Africa is only six of ten. Even worse, just 31 percent of secondary school–age teenagers are attending classes in sub-Saharan Africa versus 74 percent in MENA.

Among the world's 30 youngest countries, only two (Afghanistan and Guatemala) are outside this region, and 27 of the remaining 28 are in sub-Saharan Africa. Yemen is the one exception and, not surprisingly, is also MENA's sole low-income nation. Sub-Saharan Africa has many such nations.

Oil is an important revenue source in both subregions, creating "haves" and "have nots" among the 73 nations. Petroleum exploration has accelerated in sub-Saharan Africa (see box on page 88), for several reasons: developed countries are anxious to reduce their dependency on the Middle East, emerging nations like China and India want to lock in secure energy sources, and exploration is less expensive in west Africa than elsewhere because drilling is in relatively shallow water. From 1995 to 2006, Africa's oil-exporting economies grew by 9.3 percent annually, as compared with growth of only 3.6 percent per year in its land-locked nations without mineral resources.

URBAN EXPANSION

The massive urban migration that has characterized this region is accelerating: urbanization is expected to rise from 44 percent in 2007 to 54 percent in 2030 and over 64 percent in 2050. Numerically, the progression is

▸▸ 1950: 33 million urban dwellers,

▸▸ 2007: 373 million urban dwellers,

▸▸ 2050: 1.3 billion urban dwellers.

Figure 6-3

Countries with Female Employment-to-Population Ratios Below 30 Percent or Above 70 Percent

MENA	Sub-Saharan Africa	Other Regions
BELOW 30 PERCENT		
Bahrain	Lesotho	Macedonia
Eqypt	Namibia	Suriname
Iraq	Sudan	
Jordan	Swaziland	
Morocco		
Oman		
Saudi Arabia		
Tunisia		
Turkey		
West Bank and Gaza		
Yemen		
OVER 70 PERCENT		
None	Burkina Faso	Cambodia
	Burundi	Vietnam
	Guinea	
	Madagascar	
	Malawi	
	Mozambique	
	Rwanda	
	Tanzania	
	Uganda	

Source: ILO, *Key Indicators of the Labor Market*, 5th edition, figure 2b.

Figure 6-4

MENA and Sub-Saharan Africa, More Contrasts than Similarities

	MENA	Sub-Saharan Africa	World
Population, 2007 (million)	338	807	6,700
Annual growth rate (percent)	1.8	2.5	1.2
Growth in working-age population 2005–2030 (percent)	52.2	90.6	29.5
Life expectancy (years)	70	50	68
Fertility rate (number of births per woman)	2.9	5.2	2.5
Primary school completion (percent)	91	60	86
Secondary school enrollment, relevant ages (percent)	74	31	65
Child immunization for measles (percent)	92	71	65
Per capita income, (2007 dollars, PPP)	$7,385	$1,870	$9,852
Population with access to improved sanitation (percent)	76	37	57
Phone subscribers (percent)	53	15	59
Internet users (percent)	14	3.8	21.4

Sources: World Bank, World Development Indicators database and *The Little Data Book*, 2008; UN Population Division, *World Urbanization Prospects: the 2007 Revision*, table A.1, and *World Population Prospects: the 2006 Revision*.

Figure 6-5

Source: UN Population
Division, *World Urbanization
Prospects: The 2007 Revision*,
tables A.1, A.2, and A.5.
http://esa.un.org/unup.

Urbanization in MENA and Sub-Saharan Africa
(PERCENT)

	PERCENTAGE URBANIZED		
	2007	2030	2050
Total Region	**43.7**	**53.9**	**64.5**
Middle East Total	60.2	68.1	76.2
Western Asia*	65.5	72.5	79.3
Northern Africa*	52.9	61.5	71.4
Sub-Saharan Africa	35.9	48.2	60.5
Selected Countries			
Egypt	42.7	49.9	62.4
Ethiopia	16.6	27.4	42.1
Gabon	84.7	90.6	93.5
Israel	91.7	93.0	94.6
Kenya	21.3	33.0	48.1
Liberia	59.5	73.7	83.1
Libya	77.3	82.9	87.2
Mauritius	42.3	51.1	63.4
Qatar	95.6	96.9	97.6
Saudi Arabia	81.4	86.2	89.7
Senegal	42.0	53.2	65.7
South Africa	60.2	71.3	79.6
Syria	53.8	64.0	73.9
Turkey	68.3	77.7	84.0
Uganda	12.8	20.6	33.5

*UN categorization of countries by region.

The infrastructure (roads, water, electricity, sanitation, solid waste management, etc.), residences, shops, and public facilities necessary to accommodate urban expansion of this magnitude boggles the mind. Provision of affordable housing is an issue in all but the highest-income countries (of which sub-Saharan Africa has none). Already, 20 to 40 percent of urban housing is in the informal sector,[2] and slums are ballooning as rural migrants arrive looking for urban jobs.

Figure 6-5 shows that sub-Saharan Africa is still predominantly rural, in contrast to North Africa, where a bare majority is urban, and western Asia (the Middle East), where nearly two-thirds of residents are in towns and cities. Places like Israel and Qatar are almost entirely urban today and Saudi Arabia, at 81 percent, is close. However, Uganda and Ethiopia are essentially rural nations. Despite Cairo's size, Egypt's urbanization rate is a modest 43 percent—about the same as Mauritius and Senegal. Nonetheless, by 2050, Egypt will add 20 percentage points to its urbanization rate and will have experienced urban growth comparable to that expected in most sub-Saharan nations.

MENA is a region of new town development, with Dubai the most extreme example. Egypt plans to create 20 new cities to divert people from Cairo, and Saudi Arabia wants five new supercities to ease Jeddah's and Riyadh's growth. New Saudi towns are typically seeded with modern industrial plants that are part of the country's economic diversification plan. Given the strong employment base, residential, retail, and service properties can be built simultaneously. The most prominent such project is the proposed $27 billion King Abdullah Economic City (KAEC, pronounced "cake"), which is 62 miles north of Jeddah along the Red Sea. In 20 years, this city is envisioned to be the size of Washington, D.C., and the intent is to use private funding for its creation.

Among the world's 19 current megacities with populations over 10 million, just two— Cairo and Istanbul—are in this region and both are in MENA. By 2025, Kinshasa in the Democratic Republic of Congo and Lagos[3] in Nigeria will be on the list of 27 megacities; and both of those sub-Saharan metropolitan areas will be larger than Cairo or Istanbul.

Figure 6-6a

Morocco: Population by Age and Sex in Five-Year Cohorts
1970, 2010, AND 2050 (PERCENT)

1970 Total Population = 15.3 million

2010 Total Population = 32.4 million

2050 Total Population = 42.6 million

DEMOGRAPHIC DETAILS

Appendix 3 presents basic demographic information for each of the 73 countries in the region—contemporary facts and figures, as well as projections. To illustrate the demographic range in this part of the world, the diagrams in figure 6-6 present the evolving profiles of three countries.

Morocco's diagrams portray the effects of drastic fertility rate reduction—from 7.2 children per woman in the early 1950s to 5.9 children in the late 1970s and down to 2.4 in 2006. By mid-century, fertility is expected to be below replacement level. With a significant concurrent increase in life expectancy, Morocco will have a much higher

Source: UN Population Division, *World Population Prospects: The 2006 Revision*, http://esa.un.org/unpp.

Figure 6-6b

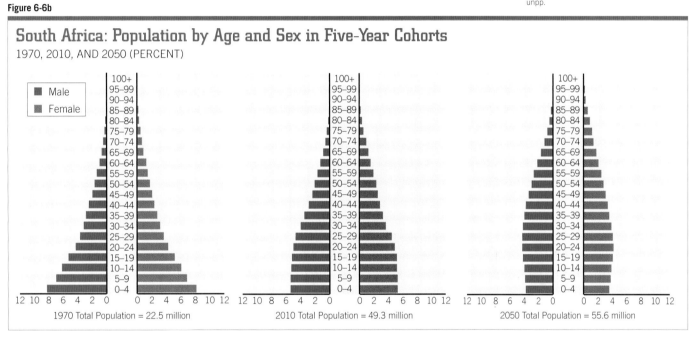

South Africa: Population by Age and Sex in Five-Year Cohorts
1970, 2010, AND 2050 (PERCENT)

1970 Total Population = 22.5 million

2010 Total Population = 49.3 million

2050 Total Population = 55.6 million

Figure 6-6c

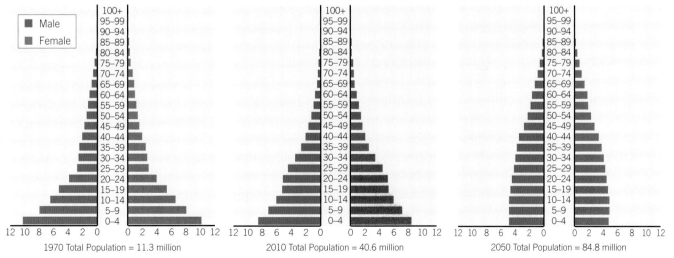

Kenya: Population by Age and Sex in Five-Year Cohorts
1970, 2010, AND 2050 (PERCENT)

1970 Total Population = 11.3 million

2010 Total Population = 40.6 million

2050 Total Population = 84.8 million

proportion of older residents. Within one lifetime, the pyramid of 1970 will become a column.

South Africa's change in profile from 1970 to today reflects the loss of young and middle-aged men and women to AIDS. The country's fertility rate decline is a bit less dramatic than Morocco's but still very significant—from 6.5 children per woman 50 years ago to 2.7 today and the likelihood of reaching replacement level by 2030. Life expectancy at birth is only 51 years, though, so the number of older citizens is modest. The proportion of working-age adults will be high at mid-century.

In direct contrast, Kenya still has a fertility rate of 5.0, so lots of children appear on the diagram. However, with an expectation that fertility will be halved by 2050, youth will no longer make up a disproportionate share of the population. The prevalence of AIDS in the adult population is about one-third that in South Africa, but early deaths have affected the current profile. Also, life expectancy is only 53 years, producing a squat diagram for 2050.

Middle East and North Africa

For many of the factors included in figure 6-4, MENA is ahead of global averages. Life expectancy is higher; primary and secondary school attendance is better; a far greater proportion of children receive measles and other immunizations; and 76 percent of the population has access to improved sanitation (compared with 57 percent worldwide). A big difference, though, is MENA's disproportionate number of youth, a situation that will require extraordinary job creation over time. To put the situation in perspective: whereas the world's population had a median age of 28 years in 2005, 15 of the 20 MENA countries had lower medians, and four of the five remaining ones had median ages of 29 years—just one year above the global figure. The youngest—Yemen and Palestine—have medians of 17 years, which means that more than half their populations are below legal age. Iraq is third youngest, with a median of 19 years, followed by Syria and Jordan at 21 years.

"Gaza and Kenya have more in common than short names ending in 'a.' . . . Both have too many people, or to be more exact, too many young men without either jobs or prospects. The resulting frustration is one of the causes of their present discontents."

—"Palestine's Politics," *The Economist*, January 31, 2008

Rapid Growth but No Infrastructure

Lagos, West Africa's commercial hub, was originally intended to house fewer than 100,000 residents and still has an infrastructure that might have worked at that size. However, today's Lagos probably qualifies as a megacity (over 10 million residents), and 6,000 newcomers reportedly arrive daily. Yet, as journalist Will Conners summarizes: "Rapid growth has added to a deeply rooted system of corruption that . . . hobbles attempts at improving infrastructure. . . . The corruption means billion-dollar electricity projects are left half done, so most of the city runs on expensive diesel-powered generators. It also means new hotel projects are left as empty shells, devoid of activity, so room rates at existing hotels are exorbitant."

Lagos ranks 30th in Mercer's study of the world's most expensive cities for expatriates, which places it slightly below New York but above Los Angeles, Miami, and Washington, D.C. Yet the average Nigerian survives on less than $2 a day, and over 70 percent of Lagos residents live in informal slum housing without electricity or water.

Ironically, the affluent live and work on the coastal islands of Lagos, which have the least infrastructure and are most threatened by a rising Atlantic Ocean. Here, the diesel generators run close to 24/7 and produce energy bills in the thousands of dollars.

Source: Will Connors, "Megacities: Reclaiming Lagos," *Time*, September 8, 2008, Global Business special section, p. 6.

Tunis, Tunisia.

DEBORAH L. BRETT

EDUCATION AND SKILLS

Literacy in the western Asia (Middle East) countries is 92 percent among 15- to 24-year-olds; North Africa's rate is 83 percent. There is considerable variation among countries, however, with high literacy in Azerbaijan, Turkey, and Tunisia; a lower rate in Egypt (which has a 12 percentage point spread between men and women); and Morocco at an even lower 71 percent youth literacy rate, with a 20 point difference between men and women.

Despite strong overall literacy rates, public education in MENA often relies on rote learning and does not prepare students for today's high-tech world. In Saudi Arabia, religious education takes precedence over secular study. Also in Egypt, Jordan, Palestine, and the Gulf countries, education is hampered by the fact that far too little seminal nonfiction writing is translated into Arabic. Therefore, pupils studying in a second language have a marked advantage over monolingual Arabic learners. This is clear across North Africa, where many people also speak and read French.

Israel has excellent universities, and strong academic institutions are scattered across the MENA region, but mass primary and secondary education remains mediocre at best. As a result, elite Arab students are typically western educated, often from high school onward.

Consistent with education issues, MENA is one-third below the global average in Internet familiarity, with 13.8 users per 100 people (see figure 6-4). Globally, 21.4 of every

Figure 6-7

MENA's Most Affluent Nations

	2007 Per Capita GNI, PPP (Dollars)
Kuwait	49,970
Bahrain	34,310
United Arab Emirates*	31,190
Cyprus	26,370
Israel	25,930
Saudi Arabia	22,910
Oman	19,740
Libya	14,710
Turkey	12,350

*2006 data.

Source: World Bank, World Development Indicators database, revised 17 October 2008.

100 people are Internet users. For this indicator, the range among MENA's nations is particularly broad. The strongest familiarity with the Internet is in the United Arab Emirates where 40.2 of every 100 people are users. Ratios in Qatar, Kuwait, Israel, and Lebanon are also above the global average. Right at the average level are Bahrain and Morocco (where back-office and call center operations for French speakers are expanding). Turkey, Jordan, Tunisia, and Oman cluster around the MENA average; and after them, usage falls to low levels. For young people with long careers ahead of them, Internet familiarity is essential.

INCOME

Thanks to oil, much of the Middle East is wealthy, albeit not the most populous nations. Figure 6-7 lists the World Bank's per capita income estimates for the region's most affluent countries. Classified as high-income locales, the top six are Kuwait, Bahrain, the United Arab Emirates, Cyprus, Israel, and Saudi Arabia. The other three are considered upper-middle-income nations. All these countries have both affluent and middle-class consumers in abundance and are consequently attracting shopping center developments, including IKEA and other global chains. Istanbul, for example, is said to have over 80 shopping malls, apart from the Grand Bazaar for which it has long been famous.

LABOR FORCE

Persian Gulf countries are major importers of labor at all skill levels, though the largest numbers of jobs are for manual laborers, clerks, and household workers. Partly because of pressure from neighboring politicians, many migrants are from Egypt, Palestine, Jordan, and Yemen; but even more are from South Asia. For the most part, these are contract laborers whose families do not accompany them. Despite hot, harsh, and lonely conditions, these workers earn multiples of what they could at home and are able to remit money to their families.

If more young men from the immediate region were employed in the Gulf, they could save enough to marry sooner. In Arab culture, where marriage is essential for men and women, tradition dictates that a man be able to buy and furnish a home before he can marry. With larger numbers of young people competing for too few jobs, men are frequently in their thirties or even forties before they are able to marry. The cumulative frustration of educated 15- to 24-year-olds without jobs or positive prospects causes the kind of social instability for which the Middle East is notorious. As reported in *The Economist*, some progress has occurred: "Ten years ago, 63 percent of Egyptian men remained unmarried at 30, a frightening indicator in a tradition-bound society where marriage is seen as a prerequisite for independence and adulthood. That figure fell to 45 percent in 2006."[4] Undoubtedly, a contributor to this improvement is the fact that 1 million of Saudi Arabia's 6 million imported workers are Egyptians.

REAL ESTATE OPPORTUNITIES

A high proportion of the world's construction cranes have recently been centered on the Middle East, with 20 percent said to have been in Dubai alone in the summer of 2008. The

Dubai: This Cycle's Development Bubble

As the Persian Gulf's commercial capital, Dubai became a luxury destination for tourists and business brokers. Its safety, sunny beaches, free-wheeling social scene, glitzy shopping centers, and easy access drew regional vacationers as well as snowbirds from Europe and Russia. Emirati represent no more than 15 percent of Dubai's population of over 1 million, so virtually all employees in Dubai and on Emirates Airline are foreign workers, originating from all over the world but with the largest numbers coming from southern Asia.

Although the government's cash cows are the enormous modern port and aluminum industries, about 30 percent of GDP depends on travel and tourism. Once foreigners were permitted to buy properties in 2002, real estate became the economy's linchpin,

with millions of residential, retail, hotel, and office square feet launched in one "look at me" architectural complex after another. Sadly, the expansion was purely investment-driven, with speculation fueling price increases. Residential units became "trading sardines" that no owner intended to occupy.

The bubble has burst, and it is hard to predict how far values will drop. The state controls the larger property developers, and there is a transparency problem. The belief is that Abu Dhabi will not allow Dubai to collapse. Nonetheless, the Emirate is likely to emerge chastened and with a lot of partially completed projects. It is hard to know when—or if—all those manmade islands will be completed.

combination of population growth, urbanization, and revenues produced by high-priced oil generated enough projects to keep global architects and construction contractors busy. In a few locations—Dubai being the most obvious—exuberance got out of hand, but most current residential and commercial development legitimately serves emerging regional economies. Though highly visible thanks to its own marketing, Dubai is unique rather than typical of the region. Its excess derives from a lack of demographically driven demand for abundant residential and office projects. Speculation fueled the bubble (see box).

Demographics certainly motivate Emirates Airline, which supports Dubai's huge and expanding airport and is an important source of economic pride and jobs. Dubai is now a dominant hub for air transit among continents: between Africa and Asia, between Europe and Africa, between Northern America and Africa or South Asia. Many transfers occur in the middle of the night, when the airport is bustling: by being brightly lit and commercially active, it fools passengers into thinking they are wide awake. Although few transiting passengers visit Dubai City, a hub of this magnitude draws regional businesses and serves the tourists the Emirate is keen to attract.

Dubai, United Arab Emirates.

FREDERICA GAMBLE

More normal real estate development in MENA is exemplified by Morocco and Turkey—emerging markets with unique political structures, distinctive histories, and regional as well as global orientations. By sending workers to Europe for generations, both have cultivated interchange with countries outside their regions. Turkey is further along the contemporary development spectrum, but Morocco was an intriguing tourist destination well before Humphrey Bogart and Ingrid Bergman appeared in "Casablanca."

MOROCCO Strategically situated at the mouth of the Mediterranean, the kingdom of Morocco just opened TangerMed, a new deepwater port with an annual capacity of 8.5 million containers. Another infrastructure focus is high-speed passenger trains using the French TGV technology. The initial, $2.7 billion line is planned to open in 2013 and will reduce the six-hour trip between Tangier and Casablanca to two hours and ten minutes. The second line will take travelers from Casablanca to Marrakech in one hour and 20

Tangier, Morocco.

minutes instead of today's three hours. These trains will enhance both business and tourist travel. Morocco attracted 7.5 million tourists in 2007—one-third of the nation's total population—and has a large expatriate community from all over the world. Within MENA, it is the fourth most popular tourist destination, after Egypt, Saudi Arabia, and the United Arab Emirates.

Since ascending the throne in 1999, King Mohammad VI has liberalized both politics and economics, with the intent of expanding as well as modernizing production. The country has become a leader in the conversion of phosphates into chemicals and fertilizers that are shipped abroad. The Green Morocco Plan is boosting agricultural productivity, with the goal of exporting more fruits and vegetables to Europe. As mentioned earlier, Morocco is increasingly providing Internet technology support to French companies. This is an economy to watch.

TURKEY With its 73 million people, Turkey is two and a half times larger than Morocco. In the middle of the last century, Turkey was an agrarian society and 80 percent of the population was rural; today, it is 70 percent urbanized. Over the past decade, urban areas added 10 million people, with one-fifth attracted to Istanbul.

The combination of newly formed households, migration, and gentrification creates demand for 700,000 residential units each year. In the words of Jones Lang LaSalle, "Turkey remains arguably the largest untapped real estate market in Europe, offering both significant size and growth potential."[5] Jones Lang LaSalle classifies Turkey's 19 cities into three tiers: the first is Istanbul, in a class by itself; the second contains five diverse cities—Ankara, Izmir, Antalya, and two satellites of Istanbul (Bursa and Kocaeli); and the third includes 13 smaller urban areas. The categorization is based on population size and growth, purchasing power, economic activity, and potential for foreign investment. Figure 6-8 summarizes Jones Lang LaSalle's enthusiastic assessment of development opportunities in the top six Turkish cities.

Among emerging markets, Turkey is akin to Mexico and South Africa in being more mature economically. Reforms introduced after the 2001 financial crisis strengthened both the banking system and the economy. Agriculture represents only 10 percent of Turkey's GDP; 27 percent is from industry and 63 percent from services. Because of its strategic geopolitical location, with Europe to the northwest, the Turkic republics and

Figure 6-8

Turkey's Urban Development Opportunities

City	Office	Retail	Residential	Logistics	Hotel
Istanbul					
Ankara					
Izmir					
Bursa					
Kocaeli					
Antalya					

Significant opportunities
Good opportunities
Selective opportunities

Source: Jones Lang LaSalle, 2008.

Russia to the northeast, and the Middle East to the south, Turkey has become a regional automotive and appliance manufacturing and distribution center. Its four major production centers are Istanbul, Izmir, Ankara, and Adana.

Civil engineering and construction have long been Turkish strengths, and its global contracting firms are active throughout the world, not just in their own region. Turkey has large REITs focused on residential and retail development—at home and abroad. Foreign investment is welcome and legal foundations are strong, so international investors are interested in Turkey.

Sub-Saharan Africa

As highlighted in figure 6-4, sub-Saharan Africa is an outlier in relation to world statistics: its 2.5 percent annual population growth rate is more than twice the globe's 1.2 percent; its working-age population will expand three times as fast; its fertility rate is twice the worldwide figure; at 50 years, its life expectancy is not even three-fourths as long as that of the average global resident; its per capita income is the lowest in the world; and so forth.

In sub-Saharan Africa, 62 percent of all employment is in agriculture, compared with one-third of global jobs. The fact that most people work on subsistence farms is both good and bad: the good news is they raise their own food, but the bad news is the farms are inefficient. Despite richly productive land in one nation after another, farmers typically do not plant the best seeds, use commercial fertilizer, share equipment with neighbors, have access to effective marketing if they produce saleable quantities, or own large enough plots for efficient production. An extremely fertile country like Uganda, for example, could be exporting far more produce to its neighbors if there were more functional agricultural cooperatives or large corporate farms.

The greater an economy's reliance on agriculture, the poorer the country, as outlined in chapter 2. When industrial and service employment rises, people move to towns and cities, school attendance goes up, and fertility rates decline. Figure 6-9 illustrates this pattern by arraying 15 countries in three relative wealth categories and showing the proportion of value added to their economies from agriculture, industry, and services. (Government work is included in services.) Clearly, the upper-middle-income African nations have only 2 to 6 percent of their GDP coming from agriculture. Botswana benefits from its diamond mines; Gabon is highly industrialized as well; the island nation of Mauritius relies on tourism and trade; and South Africa has a very diverse economy based on resource extraction, manufacturing, services, and finance.

The three lower-middle-income countries rely more on agriculture—but not as much as the low-income nations. Angola is an oil producer, which explains the 70 percent of GDP derived from industry. Nigeria is also oil rich, but the combination of its large size, high fertility, and rampant corruption keep it poor. Two other very large countries—Ethiopia and the Democratic Republic of Congo—still depend on agriculture for half their GDPs.

Uganda reduced its reliance on agriculture dramatically between 1990 and 2006— from 57 down to 32 percent, partly thanks to the discovery of oil. The two other countries with notable but much smaller reductions in agriculture's importance are Guinea and

"Peter Rammutla, president of the National African Farmer's Union, . . . said in 2003 that Africa's crop production was the lowest in the world, at 1.7 tons per 1 hectare (about 2.5 acres) compared with 4 tons globally. Its productivity has stagnated for decades while Asian yield has tripled and Latin American yield has doubled. Although genetically modified foods were initially very controversial in Africa, as in other parts of the world, the need for inexpensive food and increased production for small farmers is leading to calls for a 'green revolution' in Africa."

—Vijay Mahajan, *Africa Rising*, p. 120

Figure 6-9

Components of Economic Value Added by Income Category, Sub-Saharan Countries

(PERCENTAGE OF 2006 GDP)

	Agriculture	Industry	Services
World	**3**	**28**	**69**
Sub-Saharan Africa	15	30	55
Upper-Middle-Income Nations			
Botswana	2	53	45
Gabon	5	61	34
Mauritius	6	27	68
South Africa	3	31	66
Lower-Middle-Income Nations			
Angola	9	70	21
Cameroon	20	33	47
Namibia	11	31	58
Low-Income Nations			
Democratic Republic of Congo	46	28	27
Ethiopia	47	13	39
Guinea	13	37	50
Kenya	27	19	54
Nigeria	23	57	20
Madagascar	28	15	57
Uganda	32	18	49
Zambia	22	33	45

Source: World Bank.

Nigeria. The countries on this list with little or no reduction from 1990 to 2006 are Namibia, Madagascar, and Zambia.

With the most youthful profile in the world, sub-Saharan Africa's working-age population represents only 54 percent of total residents. The proportion will rise to 60 percent by 2030—still the world's lowest rate but brushing up against western Europe, where all the senior citizens erode the working-age percentage. If the two regions could be merged, African children and European elders would bracket workers and create a normal age/sex diagram.

Fanciful though that image is, Africa's young people will need to assume a higher proportion of the world's work as time goes on. When commodity demand picks up again, global attention will return to Africa. China is currently an active investor, anxious to secure copper, iron ore, oil, natural gas, uranium, and the like. In return, the Chinese invest in infrastructure projects and assist mineral-rich nations with economic development. India began the same process more recently, emphasizing the long trading history between the continents and pointing to the 2 million ethnic Indians residing in Africa. The United States imports African oil as a way of paring down its reliance on the Middle East; already, more oil is imported to America from Africa than from Saudi Arabia.

Inadequate education is a constraint for many young Africans seeing employment. Except for the southern subregion and very small, anomalous countries like Equatorial Guinea and Mauritius, literacy is low across sub-Saharan Africa. Burkina Faso and Niger, which have populations of 14 million apiece, have literacy rates of 31 and 36 percent respectively—among the lowest on earth. Not surprisingly, both these low-income western African nations have extremely high fertility rates—6.1 children per woman in Burkina Faso and 7.0 in Niger. Ironically, Niger is the world's fifth largest uranium producer, but its resources have not yet benefited the populace.

Africa's Retail Potential

Africa's 900 million residents can be divided into three consumer groups:

▸▸ **AFRICA ONE** makes up 5 to 15 percent (50 to 150 million people). These elite shoppers with the most disposable income were the early targets of global retailers and remain very important to malls, car dealers, restaurants, airlines, and residential developers.

▸▸ **AFRICA TWO** represents 35 to 50 percent (350 to 500 million people). This is the future middle class who "are aspiring to a better standard of living and are upwardly mobile" (p. 58). They are the ideal shoppers of mass merchandisers who want to create customer loyalty.

▸▸ **AFRICA THREE** is the remaining 50 to 60 percent (500 to 600 million people). These very price-sensitive shoppers use informal markets and buy small quantities of unbranded goods.

Retailers are finding more buying power in Africa than published income data would support. One reason is the informal economy, which accounts for the majority of employment and may be 40 percent of gross national product across the continent—lower in South Africa and higher in Tanzania. In addition, as much as 5 percent of Africa's GNI may be remittances from workers abroad; labor migration from one African country to another is on the increase, along with migration to other continents.

The youthful population triggers demand for products from diapers to school uniforms and prompts expenditures on entertainment and sports. Thanks to cell phones, television, and the Internet, young people are leapfrogging onto the global stage and, unlike older politicians, are not burdened by memories of colonialism. "With the right product at the right price [and in the right size], there is a very attractive market in Africa" (p. 56).

Source: Vijay Mahajan, *Africa Rising*.

Much of Africa's economic news is positive. As indicated earlier, industry and trade are expanding within and among countries, foreign investment is accelerating mineral extraction and contributing to port development, entrepreneurs are flourishing, and naturally optimistic people are beginning to feel more like realists. Finance and telecommunication innovations have been key economic drivers. Cell phones are especially helpful to farmers and traders, but they vastly improve overall efficiency in places that did not have land lines or high enough literacy to rely on mail service. In 1998, there were an estimated 2 million cell phones in Africa; ten years later, there were at least 130 million—and far more users than phones, because people share equipment and pay one another and "cell phone kiosk ladies" for individual calls.

It is hard to overstate the boost this technology has given the economy. In Kenya, four times more people have cell phones than bank accounts. With Nokia selling new phones for as little as $33, 10 million residents have low-cost phones. Two years ago, Safaricom introduced a program by which money can be sent by phone.[6] Not only does this enhance trade, but it enables urban workers to remit funds to their rural families on a more regular basis. Infrastructure and transportation are still huge challenges across Africa and from north to south: moving goods among countries is not easy, but roads and barge routes are being developed.

The International Monetary Fund says there is enough stability in eight sub-Saharan countries to qualify them as emerging markets:

- Botswana,
- Ghana,
- Kenya,
- Mozambique,
- Nigeria,
- Tanzania,
- Uganda, and
- Zambia.

Lists like this vary among agencies. The World Bank prefers to talk about nine middle-income countries: Cape Verde, Equatorial Guinea, Gabon, Mauritius, Namibia, Seychelles, and Swaziland. South Africa is the ninth, though it is really a separate case—an already emerged market that produces one-third of sub-Saharan Africa's GDP. When Nigeria's output is added to South Africa's, the two countries account for half the GDP south of the Sahara.

Chinese-African Linkages

China established diplomatic ties with some African countries 50 years ago and was selling bicycles to Tanzania in the early 1980s, but the contemporary assault on the continent in search of commodities is at a different order of magnitude. By 2007

- 800 Chinese companies were operating in 49 countries.

- Over 230,000 Chinese visited Africa, many as tourists.

- Two-way trade reached $73 billion.

- Economic activity focused on infrastructure, public works, oil, and mining.

- Official estimates were that 750,000 Chinese were working in Africa in four major categories:
  - Temporary migrant laborers linked to Chinese developments (the largest group),
  - Small-time entrepreneurs,
  - In-transit migrants intending to reach other parts of the world, and
  - Agricultural workers.

Modest migration to China is also occurring—to study at universities, to cultivate trade relationships, for diplomacy, and for employment.

Source: Melia Politzer, "China and Africa: Stronger Economic Ties Mean More Migration," August 2008. www.migrationinformation.org/feature/display.cfm?ID=690.

Endnotes

Chapter 1

1   Northern America, as defined by the United Nations and as used in this report, includes the United States, Canada, Bermuda, and Greenland.

2   For a definition of developed nations, see appendix 1.

3   According to the UN regional definitions, many Middle Eastern nations are in Western Asia, and Algeria, Egypt, Libya, Morocco, Sudan, Tunisia, and Western Sahara are in Northern Africa. In this book, the authors group the countries as MENA—the Middle East and North Africa.

4   In 2003, the UN General Assembly defined 50 countries as "least developed," of which 34 are in Africa, ten in Asia, one in Latin America and the Caribbean, and five in Oceania.

5   UN Population Division, *World Urbanization Prospects: The 2007 Revision*, p. 1.

6   UN-HABITAT, *State of the World's Cities 2008/2009: Harmonious Cities*, p. 24.

7   World Bank, "World Urban Forum Seeks More Livable, Sustainable Cities," October 30, 2008, http://web.worldbank.org/WBSITE/EXTERNAL/NEWS/0,,print:Y~contentMDK:21958749.

8   *Harmonious Cities*, p. 141.

9   G. McGranahan, D. Balk, and B. Anderson, "The Rising Tide: Assessing the Risks of Climate Change and Human Settlements in Low-Elevation Coastal Zones," pp. 17–37.

10 McKinsey Global Institute, *Talkin' 'Bout My Generation: The Economic Impact of Aging U.S. Baby Boomers.*

11 *Ibid.*

12 In a demographic quirk, Generation Y covers 17 years, whereas the boomer cohort encompasses 18 years. If Generation Y were extended one year back or forward, it would be larger than the baby boomer generation today.

13 Douglas S. Massey, *New Faces in New Places*, p. 17.

14 Emilio A. Parrado and William Kandel, "New Hispanic Migrant Destinations: A Tale of Two Industries," in *New Faces in New Places*, p. 119.

15 Jeffrey S. Passel and D'Vera Cohn, "Undocumented Immigration Now Trails Legal Inflow, Reversing Decade-Long Trend," Pew Research Center Publications, October 2, 2008, http://pewresearch.org/pubs/978/undocumented-immigration.

16 D'Vera Cohn and Rich Morin, "American Mobility: Movers, Stayers, Places and Reasons," Pew Research Center, December 17, 2008. http://pewresearch.org/pubs/1058/american-mobility-moversstayers-places-and-reasons.

17 "Japan's Property Markets: Building Wealth," *The Economist,* January 5, 2008, p. 73.

18 Janamitra Devan, Stefano Negri, and Jonathan R. Woetzel, "Meeting the Challenges of China's Growing Cities," *The McKinsey Quarterly*, July 2008, http://www.mckinseyquarterly.com/article_print.aspx?L2=7&L3=8&ar=2152.

Chapter 2

1   When children under age 15 make up no more than 30 percent of the population and seniors 65 and older do not exceed 15 percent.

2   ILO, *Global Employment Trends, January 2009*, p. 9.

3   *Ibid.*

4   Sandra Lawson, "Women Hold Up Half the Sky," p. 7.

5   *Ibid*, p. 9.

6   UNESCO, *Overcoming Inequality: Why Governance Matters*, 2008.

7   Eric D. Beinhocker, Diana Farrell, and Ezra Greenberg, "Why Baby Boomers Will Need to Work Longer."

8   Australia, Canada, Ireland, New Zealand, the United Kingdom, and the United States.

9   World Bank, *World Development Report 2009: Reshaping Economic Geography*, p. 168.

10 *Ibid*, p. 161.

11 Mitra Toosi, "A Century of Change: The U.S. Labor Force, 1950–2050," *Monthly Labor Review*, vol. 125, no. 5, 2002, pp. 15–28.

12 Marlene A. Lee and Mark Mather, "U.S. Labor Force Trends," p. 4.

13 *Ibid.*, p. 5.

14 Louis Uchitelle, "Women Are Now Equal as Victims of Poor Economy," *The New York Times*, July 22, 2008.

15 Sarah R. Crissey, *Educational Attainment in the United States: 2007,* U.S. Census Bureau, Current Population Reports P20-560, January 2009, table 3, p. 9.

16 Michael Mandel, "Which Way to the Future?" *Business Week*, August 20 and 27, 2007, p. 45.

17 Bureau of Labor Statistics, *Employment and Earnings Online,* January 2008. Data are for persons age 16 and older. http://www.bls.gov/opub/ee/home/htm.

18 PRB, "2007 U.S. Population Data Sheet: A Profile of the Labor Force with a Focus on Scientists and Engineers," p. 5.

19 David A. Rosenberg, "A Made-in-America Manufacturing Renaissance," p. 1.

Chapter 3

1 World Bank, *Global Purchasing Power: Parities and Real Expenditures*, pp. 10–11.

2 World Bank, World Development indicators database.

3 U.S. Central Intelligence Agency, *The World Factbook*, updated 18 December 2008, http://www.cia.gov/library/publications/the-world-factbook/index.html.

4 OECD, *Growing Unequal? Income Distribution and Poverty in OECD Countries.*

5 Euromonitor International, "Russia's Growing Elite."

6 Jim O'Neill, "The Expanding Middle: The Exploding World Middle Class and Falling Global Inequality."

7 Knowledge@Wharton, "The New Global Middle Class: Potentially Profitable—But Also Unpredictable," July 9, 2008, http://knowledge.wharton.upenn.edu./article.cfm?articleid=2011.

8 Robert Frank, "Ranks of the Rich March from West to East." Calculations from Capgemini and Merrill Lynch, based on financial assets, not including the value of collectibles, primary residences, or consumer durables.

9 U.S. Census Bureau, *Income, Poverty, and Health Insurance Coverage in the United States: 2007.* Data from the Current Population Survey.

10 ILO, *Key Indicators of the Labour Market Programme*, section 9 (KILM 20).

11 FAO, *The State of Food Insecurity in the World: 2008*, Technical Annex, table 1, pp. 50–51.

12 The Food and Agricultural Organization of the United Nations indicates that its Food Price Index rose 28 percent between October 2006 and October 2008. Prices for seed and fertilizer more than doubled. See "Number of Hungry People Rises to 963 Million," press release issued 9 December 2008, http://www.fao.org/news/story/en/item/8836.

13 Certified General Accountants Association of Canada, "Where Does the Money Go: The Increasing Reliance on Household Debt in Canada," p. 18.

14 OECD Economic Outlook 83 database, annex table 23.

15 Edmund Conway, "British Household Debt is Highest in History."

16 Evan Ramstad, "South Korea's High Household Debt Adds Financial Woes."

17 Choe Sang-Hun, "The Korean Card Trick: Picking One," p. C-4.

18 Mark Landler, "Outside U.S., Credit Cards Tighten Grip."

19 Sonalde Desai and Amaresh Dubey, "Baniya, Babu, and Borrowing: Household Debt is Concerning."

Chapter 4

1 Hana Ben-Shabat et al., *Emerging Opportunities for Global Retailers: The A. T. Kearney 2008 Global Retail Development Index*, p. 1.

2 Mike Moriarty et al., *Growth Opportunities for Global Retailers: The A. T. Kearney 2007 Global Retail Development Index*, pp. 17–19.

3 Phil Kim, "Asia's Retail Revolution," p. 88.

4 Tiffany Kanaga, "The Retail Revolution: India in Fashion."

5 As quoted in Paul Strum, "European Retailing Booms," p. 23.

6 European Shopping Centre Trust and the International Council of Shopping Centers, "The Importance of Shopping Centres to the European Economy," pp. 6–7.

7 *Ibid.*, p. 7.

8 CB Richard Ellis, "Market View: Central & Eastern European Retail," p. 2.

9 Andrew E. Kramer, "In Siberia, Shopping Malls are Sprouting All Over."

10 Curt Hazlett, "Malls are Making Headway in Egypt, the Middle East's Most Under-Retailed Nation."

11 CB Richard Ellis Global Retail Research, "Global Emerging Markets Survey: A Survey of International Retailer Attitudes to Emerging Markets," p. 5.

12 "Job Losses and Income Declines Widely Anticipated," Reuters/University of Michigan Surveys of Consumers, press release for January 2009 survey.

13 U.S. Census Bureau, "Estimates of Monthly Retail and Food Services Sales by Kind of Business." Calculations based on preliminary 2008 numbers. http://www.census.gov/mrts/www/data/excel/mrts-sales92-08.xls. See also "E-Stats," 4th Quarter 2008, tables 1 and 3 (preliminary). http://www.census.gov/mrts/www/ecomm.html. E-Stats are based on total sales, including automotive.

14 Forbes.com, "The Mall Pall."

Chapter 5

1 In February, the Czech Republic offered a free plane ticket and $649 to foreign workers who had lost their jobs and agreed to go home.

2 According to the Alan Guttmacher Institute, 44 abortions were performed in 2003 per 1,000 women age 15 to 44 in eastern Europe (45 in Russia), compared with only 12, 17, and 18 in western, northern, and southern Europe respectively. Even so, the abortion rate in all of eastern Europe had dropped by more than half between 1995 and 2003; Russia registered a 49 percent drop. Analysts attribute these dramatic decreases to improved contraception, not a desire for more children. The United States abortion rate—23 per 1,000—remained essentially unchanged.

3 Sara Rhodin, "A Holiday and a Park Bench From Russia With Love."

4 Russell Shorto, "No Babies."

5 Ian Fisher, "In a Funk, Italy Sings an Aria of Disappointment," p. 1.

6 Molly Moore, "As Europe Grows Grayer, France Devises a Baby Boom," p. A01.

7 Nicholas Kulish, "Falling German Birthrate Dispels Baby Miracle Myth"; PRB, "2008 World Population Data Sheet."

8 Agence France-Presse, AFP News, January 13, 2009.

9 Jeffrey Stinson, "Euro-Babies Go from Bust to Boom."

10 "Suddenly the Old World Looks Younger," *The Economist*, p. 31.

11 http://www.citypopulation.de.

12 Peter Gumbel, "London Falling."

13 "The Rivals," *The Economist*. Foreign-born persons are estimated to constitute 30 percent of the population of London, compared with 14 percent in Paris.

14 Russia is not part of the European Union and is generally omitted from its statistical series.

15 Courtney Weaver, "Cigarettes Killing Russia Softly," p. 2. Sixty percent of Russian men smoke. Tobacco taxes are low.

16 Carter Dougherty, "After Enacting Pension Cuts, Europe Weathers a Storm."

17 "Top 10 Migration Issues of 2008: Issue #1 – 'Buyer's Remorse' on Immigration Policy," Migration Policy Institute, December 4, 2008. http://www.migrationinformation.org.

18 Victoria Burnett, "Jobless Migrants Struggle as Spain's Economy Cools," p. A14.

19 *Ibid.*; Thomas Catan, "Spain's Job Crisis Leaves Immigrants Out of Work," p. A5.

20 Migration Policy Institute, *op. cit.*

21 Elisabeth Rosenthal, "Italy Arrests Hundreds of Immigrants"; Rachel Donadio, "Italy's Attacks on Migrants Fuel Debate on Racism," p. A5.

22 "Two Unamalgamated Worlds," *The Economist*.

23 OECD, *OECD Factbook 2008: Economic, Environmental, and Social Statistics*.

24 Royal Institution of Chartered Surveyors, *2009 Housing Forecast*, p. 1.

Chapter 6

1 The UN does not break out the Middle East as a separate subregion; this area is Western Asia in their terminology. It therefore includes Cyprus, which is actually in the European Union, Turkey, Armenia, and Azerbaijan, as well as all the countries generally considered the Middle East. We use "the Middle East" throughout this report.

2 Informal housing includes "illegal" dwellings that do not meet building or zoning codes, often lack utilities, and have neither deeds nor leases. Some units in Lagos offer little more than a roof over a sleeping space. In South Africa, many informal units are in the backyards of legal residences.

3 Lagos probably qualifies as a megacity already but, with an estimated 70 percent of the population living in informal housing, accurate counts are difficult.

4 "Egypt: Will the Dam Burst?," p. 32.

5 Jones Lang LaSalle, *Turkey's Rising Stars*, p. 4.

6 "Companies like Wizzit, in South Africa, and GCash, in the Philippines, have started programs that allow customers to use their phones to store cash credits transferred from another phone or purchased through a post office, phone-kiosk operator or other licensed operator" (Sara Corbett, "Can the Cellphone Help End Global Poverty?" p. 39).

Bibliography

Beinhocker, Eric D., Diana Farrell, and Ezra Greenberg. "Why Baby Boomers Will Need to Work Longer." *The McKinsey Quarterly*, November 2008. www.mckinseyquarterly.com/article_print. aspx?L2=7&L3=8&ar=2234.

Ben-Shabat, Hana, Mike Moriarty, Ram Kuppuswamy, and Mohammad Alam. Emerging *Opportunities for Global Retailers: The 2008 A. T. Kearney Global Retail Development Index*. Chicago: A.T. Kearney, 2008.

Burnett, Victoria. "Jobless Migrants Struggle as Spain's Economy Cools." *The New York Times*, December 10, 2008.

Carbaugh, Robert J. "Is International Trade a Substitute for Migration?" *Global Economy Journal*, vol. 7, no. 3, 2007.

Catan, Thomas. "Spain's Job Crisis Leaves Immigrants Out of Work." *The Wall Street Journal*, January 24–25, 2009.

CB Richard Ellis. "MarketView: Central & Eastern Europe Retail." Autumn 2008. http://www.cbre.eu/ research.

CB Richard Ellis, Europe, Middle East, and Africa Research. "How Global Is the Business of Retail?" 2008. http://www.cbre.com.

CB Richard Ellis, Global Retail Research. "Global Emerging Markets Survey: A Survey of International Retailer Attitudes to Emerging Markets." Summary Report. 2008. http://www.cbre.eu.

Certified General Accountants Association of Canada. "Where Does the Money Go: The Increasing Reliance on Household Debt in Canada." Toronto, 2007.

Choe, Sang-Hun. "The Korean Card Trick: Picking One." *The New York Times*, January 1, 2008.

Conway, Edmund. "British Household Debt Is Highest in History." *The Telegraph*, June 6, 2008.

Corbett, Sara. "Can the Cellphone Help End Global Poverty?" *The New York Times Magazine*, April 13, 2008.

Desai, Sonalde, and Amaresh Dubey. "Baniya, Babu, and Borrowing: Household Debt Is Concerning." *The Economic Times*, October 3, 2007.

Donadio, Rachel. "Italy's Attacks on Migrants Fuel Debate on Racism." *The New York Times,* October 13, 2008.

Dougherty, Carter. "After Enacting Pension Cuts, Europe Weathers a Storm." *The New York Times*, August 6, 2008.

Economic Commission for Latin America and the Caribbean. *Statistical Yearbook 2007*. Santiago, Chile: ECLAC, 2008.

Economist Intelligence Unit and Western Union. "The Global Migration Barometer." Washington, D.C., September 2008.

Ernst & Young. "2007 Aging U.S. Workforce Survey: Challenges and Responses—An Ongoing Review." New York, October 2007. http://www.ey.com.

Euromonitor International. "Russia's Growing Elite." August 13, 2008. http://www.euromonitor.com.

European Shopping Centre Trust and the International Council of Shopping Centers. "The Importance of Shopping Centres to the European Economy." March 2008.

FAO (Food and Agricultural Organization). *The State of Food Insecurity in the World: 2008*. Rome: FAO, 2008. http://www.fao.org.

Farrell, Diana. "China's Urbanization Means Rich Rewards for Business." *Business Week*, September 12, 2008. www.mckinsey.com/mginews/China_urban_ rich_reward.asp.

Farrell, Diana, ed. *Offshoring:Understanding the Emerging Global Labor Market*. McKinsey Global Institute. Boston: Harvard Business School Press, 2006.

Fisher, Ian. "In a Funk, Italy Sings an Aria of Disappointment." *The New York Times*, December 13, 2007.

Forbes.com. "The Mall Pall." December 11, 2008. www.forbes.com.

Frank, Robert. "Ranks of the Rich March From West to East." *The Wall Street Journal*, June 25, 2008.

Gumbel, Peter. "London Falling." *Time*, October 23, 2008.

Hazlett, Curt. "Malls Are Making Headway in Egypt, the Middle East's Most Under-Retailed Nation." *Shopping Centers Today*, International Council of Shopping Centers, 2008.

ILO (International Labour Organization). *Global Employment Trends, January 2009*. Geneva: ILO, 2009.

———. *Key Indicators of the Labour Market*. 5th edition. Geneva: ILO, 2007. http://www.ilo.org/public/english/employment/strat/kilm/download/kilm20.pdf.

Jackson, Richard and Neil Howe. *The Graying of the Great Powers: Demography and Geopolitics in the 21st Century*. Washington, D.C.: Center for Strategy and International Studies, 2008.

Jones Lang LaSalle. "Turkey's Rising Stars: A Region of New Opportunities." Global Foresight Series. London, 2008.

Kanaga, Tiffany. "The Retail Revolution: India in Fashion." *Chazen Web Journal of International Business*. April 4, 2008. http://www4.gsb.columbia.edu/chazen/journal.

Kim, Phil. "Asia's Retail Revolution." *Urban Land*, vol. 67, no. 1, January 2008.

Kramer, Andrew E. "In Siberia, Shopping Malls are Sprouting All Over." *The New York Times*, May 17, 2008.

Kulish, Nicholas. "Falling German Birthrate Dispels Baby Miracle Myth." *The New York Times*, September 23, 2007.

Landler, Mark. "Outside U.S., Credit Cards Tighten Grip." *The New York Times*, August 20, 2008.

Lawson, Sandra. "Women Hold Up Half the Sky," Goldman Sachs Global Economics Paper No. 164, New York, March 4, 2008.

Lawson, Sandra, Roopa Purushothaman, and David Heacock. "60 Is the New 55: How the G6 Can Mitigate the Burden of Aging." Goldman Sachs Global Economics Paper No. 132, New York, September 28, 2005.

Lee, Marlene A., and Mark Mather. "U.S. Labor Force Trends." *Population Bulletin*, vol. 63, no. 2, June 2008.

Mahajan, Vijay. *Africa Rising: How 900 Million African Consumers Offer More Than You Think*. New Jersey: Wharton School Publishing, 2008.

Massey, Douglas S., ed. *New Faces in New Places: the Changing Geography of American Immigration*. New York: Russell Sage Foundation, 2008.

Martel, Laurent, Eric Caron-Malenfant, Samuel Vezina, and Alain Belanger. "Labour Force Projection for Canada, 2006–2031." *Canadian Economic Observer*, June 2007. Statistics Canada Catalogue no. 11-010.

McGranahan, G., D. Balk, and B. Anderson. "The Rising Tide: Assessing the Risks of Climate Change and Human Settlements in Low-Elevation Coastal Zones." *Environment and Urbanization*, vol. 19, no. 1, 2007.

McKinsey Global Institute. *Preparing for China's Urban Billion*. San Francisco: March 2008. http://www.mckinsey.com/mgi/publications/china_urban_billion.

McKinsey Global Institute. *Talkin' 'Bout My Generation: The Economic Impact of Aging U.S. Baby Boomers*. San Francisco, June 2008. http://www.mckinsey.com/mgi/publications/Impact_Aging_Baby_Boomers.

Migration Policy Institute. "Top 10 Migration Issues of 2008: Issue #1 – Buyer's Remorse on Immigration Policy." December 4, 2008. http://www.migrationinformation.org.

Moore, Molly. "As Europe Grows Grayer, France Devises a Baby Boom." *The Washington Post,* October 18, 2006.

Morgenson, Gretchen. "Given a Shovel, Americans Dig Deeper Into Debt." *The New York Times*, July 20, 2008.

Moriarty, Mike, et al. *Growth Opportunities for Global Retailers: The A. T. Kearney 2007 Global Retail Development Index*. Chicago, 2007.

Naim, Moses. "Middle Class Rising." *The Los Angeles Times*, February 8, 2008.

National Endowment for the Arts. *Artists in the Workforce 1990–2005*. Washington, D.C., June 2008. http://www.nea.gov/research/ArtistsInWorkforce.pdf.

National Institute on Aging, U.S. Department of State. *Why Population Aging Matters: A Global Perspective*. Washington, D.C., March 2007.

O'Neill, Jim. "The Expanding Middle: The Exploding World Middle Class and Falling Global Inequality." Goldman Sachs, New York, July 2008.

OECD (Organisation for Economic Co-operation and Development). *Growing Unequal: Income Distribution and Poverty in OECD Countries*. Paris: OECD, 2008.

———. *OECD Factbook 2008: Economic, Environmental, and Social Statistics*. Paris: OECD, 2008. http://titania.sourceoecd.org/vl=9531360/cl=17/nw=1/rpsv/factbook/010304.htm.

PRB (Population Reference Bureau). "2007 U.S. Population Data Sheet: A Profile of the Labor Force with a Focus on Scientists and Engineers." Washington, D.C., May 2007. http://www.prb.org.

———. "2008 World Population Data Sheet." Washington, D.C., August 2008. http://www.prb.org.

———. "The World's Youth: 2006 Data Sheet," Washington, D.C., 2006. http://www.prb.org.

Purvis, Andrew. "Marseille's Ethnic Bouillabaisse." *Smithsonian*, December 2007.

Ramstad, Evan. "South Korea's High Household Debt Adds Financial Woes." *The Wall Street Journal*, November 29, 2008.

Rhodin, Sara. "A Holiday and a Park Bench From Russia With Love." *The New York Times*, July 9, 2008.

Rosenberg, David A. "A Made-in-America Manufacturing Renaissance." *Merrill Lynch Economic Commentary*, April 25, 2008.

Rosenthal, Elisabeth. "Italy Arrests Hundreds of Immigrants." *The New York Times*, May 16, 2008.

Royal Institution of Chartered Surveyors. "2009 Housing Forecast." Coventry, United Kingdom, December 24, 2008. http://www.rics.org.

Sachs, Jeffrey D. *Common Wealth: Economics for a Crowded Planet.* New York: The Penguin Press, 2008.

Schoenfeld, Amy. "What the World Owes." *The New York Times*, July 20, 2008.

Sedano, Fernando. "Economic Implications of Mexico's Sudden Demographic Transition." *Business Economics*, July 2008.

Shorto, Russell. "No Babies." *The New York Times Magazine*, June 29, 2008.

Stinson, Jeffrey. "Euro-babies Go from Bust to Boom." *USA Today*, August 17–18, 2007.

Strum, Paul. "European Retailing Booms." *Urban Land*, vol. 66, no. 1, January 2007.

"The Rivals." *The Economist*, March 13, 2008.

"Two Unamalgamated Worlds." *The Economist*, April 3, 2008.

Torche, Florencia, and Seymour Spilerman. "Household Wealth in Latin America," in James B. Davies (ed.), *Personal Assets from a Global Perspective.* Cambridge, United Kingdom: Cambridge University Press, 2007.

UN-Habitat (United Nations Human Settlements Programme). *State of the World's Cities 2008/2009: Harmonious Cities.* London: UN-Habitat, 2008.

UNESCO (United Nations Educational, Scientific, and Cultural Organization). *Education for All Global Monitoring Report 2009.* Paris: UNESCO, 2008.

UN Population Division, Department of Economic and Social Affairs. "World Fertility Patterns 2007." New York, 2008.

———. *World Urbanization Prospects: The 2007 Revision.* New York, February 2008.

———. "World Youth Report 2007: Young People's Transition to Adulthood—Progress and Challenges." New York, 2007.

U.S. Bureau of Labor Statistics. "Employment, Hours, and Earnings from the Current Employment Statistics Survey." http://data.bls.gov.

———. "May 2007 National Industry-Specific Occupational Employment and Wage Estimates, NAICS 445100 (Grocery Stores)." http://www.bls.gov/oes/2007/may/naics4_445100.htm.

U.S. Census Bureau. "Estimates of Monthly Retail and Food Services Sales by Kind of Business." http://www.census.gov.

———. "Income, Poverty, and Health Insurance Coverage in the United States: 2007." Washington, D.C., August 2008.

University of Pennsylvania, Wharton School. "The New Global Middle Class: Potentially Profitable—But Also Unpredictable." July 9, 2008. http://knowledge.wharton.upenn.edu/article.cfm?articleid=2011.

Walter, Megan, and David Cheadle. "Indonesia—At the Crossroads." Cushman & Wakefield Business Analytics Group, Asia Pacific, November 2008.

Weaver, Courtney. "Cigarettes Killing Russia Softly." *The International Herald-Tribune*, September 8, 2008.

World Bank. *Global Purchasing Power: Parities and Real Expenditures: 2005 International Comparison Program.* Washington, D.C.: IBRD/World Bank, 2008.

———. *The Little Data Book: 2008.* Washington, D.C.: World Bank, 2008.

———. *World Development Indicators.* Database revised October 17, 2008. http://www.worldbank.org.

———. *World Development Report 2009: Reshaping Economic Geography.* Washington, D.C.: World Bank, 2009.

Appendices

Appendix 1. Definitions

REGIONS

Unless otherwise specified, this book uses the UN categorizations of world regions:

MORE DEVELOPED REGIONS: They comprise all subregions of Europe plus Northern America, Australia and New Zealand, and Japan.

LESS DEVELOPED REGIONS: They comprise all subregions of Africa, the Middle East, Asia (excluding Japan), Latin America, and the Caribbean plus Melanesia, Micronesia, and Polynesia.

ASIA: The UN categorizes countries in four Asian subregions. In chapters 1 and 6, the Western Asia subregion has been included in the discussion of Africa and the Middle East.

AFRICA AND THE MIDDLE EAST: This area has two main subregions—sub-Saharan Africa and the Middle East and North Africa (MENA). MENA comprises countries in Western Asia (see above) and North Africa. The UN classifies Sudan as a North African country. In this book, it is classified in East Africa and sub-Saharan Africa.

ECONOMIC INDICATORS

GROSS DOMESTIC PRODUCT (GDP) is the sum of value added by all resident producers. Growth is calculated from constant price GDP data in local currency. GDP per capita is gross domestic product divided by mid-year population.

GROSS NATIONAL INCOME (GNI) measures the total domestic and foreign value-added claimed by residents. GNI comprises GDP plus net receipts of primary income (compensation of employees and property income) from nonresident sources. When calculating GNI in U.S. dollars from GNI reported in national currencies, the World Bank follows its Atlas conversion method, using a three-year average of exchange rates to smooth the effects of transitory exchange rate fluctuations. GNI differs from GDP by adjusting for income received by residents from abroad for labor and capital, for similar payments to nonresidents, and by incorporating various technical adjustments including those related to exchange rate changes over time.

PER CAPITA GNI PURCHASING POWER PARITY (PPP) is GNI converted to international dollars using PPP rates. An international dollar has the same purchasing power over GNI as a U.S. dollar has in the United States. This indicator measures the total output of goods and services for final use produced by residents and nonresidents in relation to the size of the population. As such, it is an indicator of the economic productivity of a nation. PPP conversion provides a standard measure that allows comparison of real price levels between countries. For all but high-income countries, the World Bank's Atlas methodology results in lower per capita incomes than the international dollar/PPP method as shown in the figure below.

World Bank Classification of Per Capita Income
2007

Countries	GNI Per Capita, Atlas Method (U.S. Dollars)	GNI Per Capita, PPP Method (International Dollars)
Worldwide	**7,958**	**9,852**
Low income	578	1,494
Lower middle income	1,887	4,543
Middle income	2,872	5,952
Upper middle income	6,987	11,868
Low and middle income	2,337	4,911
High income	37,566	36,100

Sources: World Bank, OECD.

Population Characteristics of European Nations with 2007 Populations of 1 Million or More

| | POPULATION (MILLIONS) | | | POPULATION CHANGE | | | |
| | | | | 2007–2030 | | 2030–2050 | |
	2007	2030	2050	Number (Millions)	Share (%)	Number (Millions)	Share (%)
EASTERN EUROPE							
Belarus	9.69	8.35	6.96	-1.34	-13.9	-1.39	-16.6
Bulgaria	7.64	6.22	4.95	-1.42	-18.5	-1.28	-20.5
Czech Republic	10.19	9.73	8.83	-0.46	-4.5	-0.90	-9.3
Hungary	10.03	9.26	8.46	-0.77	-7.7	-0.80	-8.6
Moldova	3.79	3.39	2.88	-0.41	-10.7	-0.51	-14.9
Poland	38.08	35.35	30.26	-2.73	-7.2	-5.09	-14.4
Romania	21.44	18.86	15.93	-2.58	-12.0	-2.93	-15.5
Russia	142.50	123.92	107.83	-18.58	-13.0	-16.08	-13.0
Slovakia	5.39	5.22	4.66	-0.17	-3.2	-0.55	-10.6
Ukraine	46.21	38.05	30.94	-8.15	-17.6	-7.12	-18.7
NORTHERN EUROPE							
Denmark	5.44	5.60	5.53	0.16	2.9	-0.07	-1.3
Estonia	1.34	1.22	1.13	-0.11	-8.3	-0.10	-7.8
Finland	5.28	5.47	5.36	0.19	3.6	-0.11	-2.0
Ireland	4.30	5.48	6.18	1.17	27.3	0.70	12.9
Latvia	2.28	2.01	1.77	-0.27	-11.6	-0.24	-12.1
Lithuania	3.39	3.02	2.65	-0.37	-10.8	-0.37	-12.2
Norway	4.70	5.37	5.73	0.67	14.2	0.37	6.8
Sweden	9.12	10.01	10.48	0.89	9.8	0.47	4.7
United Kingdom	60.77	66.16	68.72	5.39	8.9	2.55	3.9
SOUTHERN EUROPE							
Albania	3.19	3.52	3.45	0.33	10.3	-0.07	-1.9
Bosnia & Herzegovina	3.94	6.35	3.16	2.42	61.4	-3.19	-50.3
Croatia	4.56	4.17	3.69	-0.39	-8.5	-0.48	-11.4
Greece	11.15	11.18	10.81	0.03	0.3	-0.37	-3.3
Italy	58.88	57.52	54.61	-1.36	-2.3	-2.91	-5.1
Macedonia	2.04	1.97	1.75	-0.07	-3.5	-0.22	-11.2
Portugal	10.62	10.61	9.98	-0.02	-0.2	-0.63	-5.9
Serbia	9.86	9.92	9.64	0.06	0.6	-0.28	-2.8
Slovenia	2.00	1.90	1.69	-0.10	-5.0	-0.21	-10.9
Spain	44.28	46.68	46.40	2.40	5.4	-0.28	-0.6
WESTERN EUROPE							
Austria	8.36	8.64	8.50	0.28	3.4	-0.14	-1.7
Belgium	10.46	10.78	10.64	0.32	3.1	-0.14	-1.3
France	61.65	66.61	68.27	4.96	8.0	1.66	2.5
Germany	82.60	79.35	74.09	-3.25	-3.9	-5.26	-6.6
Netherlands	16.42	17.14	17.24	0.72	4.4	0.09	0.5
Switzerland	7.48	8.10	8.43	0.62	8.3	0.33	4.1

Sources: Population and urbanization—UN Population Division, *World Urbanization Prospects: The 2007 Revision*, tables A.1, A.2, and A.5. Median age and population age 15 to 64—U. S. Bureau of the Census, International Data Base, table 094. Labor force participation rate—*UN World Statistics Pocketbook: 2007*. Per capita income PPP—World Bank.

PERCENTAGE OF URBAN DWELLERS		MEDIAN AGE		PERCENTAGE OF POPULATION AGE 15 TO 64		LABOR FORCE PARTICIPATION RATE, 2006 (%)		PER CAPITA INCOME, 2007 PPP
2007	2030	2008	2030	2008	2030	Men	Women	($)
73.0	81.1	38.4	44.9	69.9	67.5	64.0	52.6	10,740
70.8	78.2	41.1	48.2	69.0	64.7	52.0	40.2	11,180
73.5	78.0	37.4	47.9	71.1	64.6	67.3	52.1	22,020
67.1	76.1	40.8	46.0	69.0	65.4	57.6	42.2	17,210
41.9	46.3	38.9	41.3	68.9	66.4	67.8	53.5	2,930
61.3	66.0	36.8	46.5	70.4	64.4	60.6	47.2	15,330
54.0	63.1	36.7	46.4	69.6	67.6	61.8	49.6	10,980
72.8	76.4	37.3	43.8	71.1	66.9	67.9	54.6	14,400
56.4	64.7	35.6	45.9	71.5	66.5	68.1	51.8	19,340
67.9	73.0	38.9	45.6	69.3	66.4	64.0	49.6	6,810
86.4	90.8	39.5	42.5	66.1	60.6	69.3	59.0	36,300
69.4	73.8	38.9	43.9	68.2	64.2	65.3	52.3	19,810
63.0	71.8	40.9	44.0	66.7	58.6	65.5	56.7	34,550
61.0	93.3	33.4	40.6	68.2	66.1	72.0	54.0	37,090
68.0	73.0	39.3	45.5	69.0	64.2	64.0	49.4	16,890
66.8	72.5	37.9	44.9	67.9	64.3	63.5	52.0	17,180
77.5	81.4	38.0	41.8	65.7	61.7	72.7	63.7	53,320
84.5	87.3	40.2	42.6	65.4	60.2	66.9	58.5	36,590
89.9	92.2	38.9	42.2	66.0	61.5	69.0	55.2	33,800
46.1	60.6	28.6	37.5	65.3	64.4	69.5	49.0	6,580
46.9	61.7	37.1	46.1	68.7	65.9	67.6	58.8	7,700
56.9	66.5	40.6	46.7	67.3	62.0	59.7	44.6	15,050
60.7	69.3	40.1	48.4	67.4	63.2	64.9	44.0	32,330
67.9	74.3	42.0	50.2	66.3	60.8	60.6	38.1	29,850
66.4	76.6	34.3	43.7	69.2	66.8	64.7	40.8	8,510
58.9	71.4	39.1	47.3	67.4	63.0	70.4	56.4	20,890
51.8	61.2	36.6	41.4	NA	NA	69.6	50.8	10,220
48.9	51.8	40.2	48.9	70.3	62.3	66.7	53.8	26,640
77.0	81.9	38.8	48.7	68.8	63.0	67.3	45.1	30,820
66.9	73.8	40.1	46.6	68.0	61.3	65.6	50.4	38,140
97.3	98.0	40.3	45.0	65.7	60.3	59.7	44.3	34,790
77.1	82.9	38.9	43.3	65.3	60.4	61.0	48.4	33,600
73.5	78.3	42.1	48.2	66.9	59.5	65.2	51.2	33,530
81.3	88.3	39.1	43.9	67.4	60.0	72.5	56.7	39,310
73.4	77.9	40.1	43.8	67.9	60.7	75.2	61.2	43,870

Population Characteristics of Middle Eastern and North African Nations with 2007 Populations of 1 Million or More

	POPULATION (MILLIONS)			POPULATION CHANGE			
				2007–2030		2030–2050	
				Number (Millions)	Share (%)	Number (Millions)	Share (%)
	2007	2030	2050				
WESTERN ASIA							
Armenia	3.00	2.84	2.46	-0.16	-5.5	-0.38	-13.4
Azerbaijan	8.47	9.60	9.40	1.13	13.4	-0.20	-2.0
Georgia	4.40	3.81	3.13	-0.59	-13.4	-0.67	-17.1
Iraq	28.99	47.38	61.94	18.38	63.4	14.57	30.1
Israel	6.93	9.16	10.53	2.23	32.2	1.37	14.9
Jordan	5.92	8.55	10.12	2.63	44.4	1.57	18.3
Kuwait	2.85	4.27	5.24	1.42	49.9	0.97	22.6
Lebanon	4.10	4.93	5.22	0.83	20.2	0.30	6.0
Oman	2.60	3.87	4.64	1.27	48.9	0.77	20.0
Palestinian Territory	4.02	7.32	10.27	3.30	82.2	2.95	40.2
Saudi Arabia	24.74	37.31	45.03	12.58	50.9	7.72	20.7
Syria	19.93	29.92	34.89	10.00	50.2	4.96	16.6
Turkey	74.88	92.47	98.95	17.59	23.5	6.48	7.0
United Arab Emirates	4.38	6.75	8.52	2.37	54.2	1.77	26.2
Yemen	22.39	40.77	58.01	18.38	82.1	17.24	42.3
NORTHERN AFRICA							
Algeria	33.86	44.73	49.61	10.87	32.1	4.88	10.9
Egypt	75.50	104.07	121.22	28.57	37.8	17.15	16.5
Libya	6.16	8.45	9.68	2.29	37.1	1.24	14.6
Morocco	31.22	39.26	42.58	8.04	25.7	3.32	8.5
Tunisia	10.33	12.53	13.18	2.20	21.3	0.65	5.2

Sources: Population and urbanization—UN Population Division, *World Urbanization Prospects: The 2007 Revision*, tables A.1, A.2, and A.5. Median age and population age 15 to 64—U. S. Bureau of the Census, International Data Base, table 094. Labor force participation rate—*UN World Statistics Pocketbook: 2007*. Per capita income PPP—World Bank.

PERCENTAGE OF URBAN DWELLERS		MEDIAN AGE		PERCENTAGE OF POPULATION AGE 15 TO 64		LABOR FORCE PARTICIPATION RATE, 2006 (%)		PER CAPITA INCOME, 2007 PPP
2007	2030	2008	2030	2008	2030	Men	Women	($)
63.8	69.1	31.7	41.7	67.1	66.1	60.3	47.7	5,900
51.8	60.1	27.7	38.2	67.6	67.5	73.2	60.8	6,260
52.6	60.2	35.5	43.5	66.8	64.8	76.4	49.3	4,770
66.6	70.5	18.9	25.3	55.7	64.0	77.5	20.1	NA
91.7	93.0	28.8	34.0	62.0	63.3	59.0	50.5	25,930
78.4	82.0	21.1	29.5	59.6	68.9	76.9	28.1	5,160
98.3	98.7	29.2	36.7	74.5	73.1	84.6	50.0	49,970
86.8	90.0	27.1	34.7	64.1	67.6	79.7	33.5	10,050
71.5	76.4	22.5	31.0	63.6	67.7	80.5	23.6	19,740
71.7	77.2	16.9	22.7	51.1	61.1	66.4	10.4	NA
81.4	86.2	23.3	30.0	62.7	68.2	80.4	18.2	22,910
53.8	64.0	20.6	29.2	60.2	68.7	88.0	39.2	4,370
68.3	77.7	26.7	35.5	66.1	68.8	76.2	27.7	12,350
77.8	82.4	29.4	36.5	79.0	79.7	92.7	40.5	NA
30.1	45.3	16.7	21.6	51.8	60.6	75.4	30.0	2,200
64.6	76.2	24.0	34.2	65.8	69.0	80.4	36.6	7,640
42.7	49.9	22.9	29.9	61.8	66.0	73.4	20.1	5,400
77.3	82.9	24.1	32.5	65.9	70.2	82.0	34.5	14,710
55.7	65.9	24.3	33.3	64.5	67.4	80.3	26.8	3,990
66.1	75.2	26.7	37.7	67.7	68.9	75.0	29.2	7,130

Population Characteristics of Sub-Saharan African Nations with 2007 Populations of 1 Million or More

	POPULATION (MILLIONS)			POPULATION CHANGE			
				2007–2030		2030–2050	
				Number (Millions)	Share (%)	Number (Millions)	Share (%)
	2007	2030	2050				
EASTERN AFRICA							
Burundi	8.51	17.23	28.32	8.72	102.5	11.08	64.
Eritrea	4.85	8.43	11.47	3.58	73.8	3.03	36.
Ethiopia	83.10	137.05	183.40	53.95	64.9	46.35	33.
Kenya	37.54	62.76	84.76	25.22	67.2	22.00	35.
Madagascar	19.68	32.93	44.45	13.25	67.3	11.52	35.
Malawi	13.93	23.55	31.94	9.63	69.1	8.39	35.
Mauritius	1.26	1.43	1.45	0.17	13.3	0.02	1.
Mozambique	21.40	31.12	39.12	9.72	45.4	8.00	25.
Rwanda	9.73	16.65	22.63	6.92	71.2	5.98	35.
Somalia	8.70	15.19	21.06	6.49	74.7	5.86	38.
Sudan	38.56	58.45	73.03	19.89	51.6	14.58	25.
Uganda	30.88	61.55	92.94	30.66	99.3	31.39	51.
Tanzania	40.45	65.52	85.08	25.06	62.0	19.56	29.
Zambia	11.92	17.87	22.87	5.95	49.9	5.00	28.
Zimbabwe	13.35	16.63	19.11	3.28	24.6	2.48	14.
MIDDLE AFRICA							
Angola	17.02	30.65	44.57	13.63	80.1	13.91	45.
Cameroon	18.55	26.89	33.14	8.34	45.0	6.25	23.
Central African Republic	4.34	6.21	7.61	1.87	43.1	1.40	22.
Chad	10.78	19.80	29.40	9.02	83.6	9.60	48.
Congo	3.77	5.82	7.56	2.06	54.6	1.74	29.
Democratic Rep. of Congo	62.64	122.73	186.84	60.10	95.9	64.10	52.
Gabon	1.33	1.79	2.08	0.46	34.6	0.29	16.
SOUTHERN AFRICA							
Botswana	1.88	2.36	2.70	0.48	25.3	0.35	14.
Lesotho	2.01	2.25	2.36	0.24	12.2	0.10	4.
Namibia	2.07	2.68	3.04	0.60	29.1	0.36	13.
South Africa	48.58	53.24	55.59	4.66	9.6	2.35	4.
Swaziland	1.14	1.26	1.36	0.12	10.8	0.10	7.
WESTERN AFRICA							
Benin	9.03	16.08	22.51	7.04	78.0	6.43	40.
Burkina Faso	14.78	26.51	37.50	11.72	79.3	11.00	41.
Côte d'Ivoire	19.26	28.09	34.70	8.83	45.8	6.62	23.
Gambia	1.71	2.77	3.65	1.06	62.1	0.88	31.
Ghana	23.48	34.23	41.88	10.76	45.8	7.65	22.
Guinea	9.37	16.17	22.71	6.80	72.6	6.54	40.
Guinea-Bissau	1.70	3.36	5.32	1.66	98.1	1.97	58.
Liberia	3.75	7.80	12.46	4.05	107.9	4.66	59.
Mali	12.34	23.25	34.23	10.91	88.5	10.98	47.
Mauritania	3.12	4.94	6.36	1.82	58.3	1.42	28.
Niger	14.23	30.84	53.16	16.62	116.8	22.32	72.
Nigeria		226.86	288.70	78.76	53.2	61.84	27.
Senegal	12.38	19.55	25.26	7.18	58.0	5.70	29.
Sierra Leone	5.87	9.59	13.52	3.73	63.5	3.93	41.
Togo	6.59	10.86	14.05	4.27	64.9	3.19	29.

Sources: Population and urbanization—UN Population Division, *World Urbanization Prospects: The 2007 Revision*, tables A.1, A.2, and A.5. Median age and population age 15 to 64—U. S. Bureau of the Census, International Data Base, table 094. Labor force participation rate—*UN World Statistics Pocketbook: 2007*. Per capita income PPP—World Bank.

PERCENTAGE OF URBAN DWELLERS		MEDIAN AGE		PERCENTAGE OF POPULATION AGE 15 TO 64		LABOR FORCE PARTICIPATION RATE, 2006 (%)		PER CAPITA INCOME, 2007 PPP
2007	2030	2008	2030	2008	2030	Men	Women	($)
10.1	19.8	17.0	17.7	52.3	53.4	93.3	92.0	330
20.2	34.4	18.1	22.3	54.6	63.3	90.3	58.2	520
16.6	27.4	17.5	22.2	52.7	60.9	89.2	70.9	780
21.3	33.0	18.1	21.7	54.7	61.0	89.5	69.6	1,540
29.1	41.4	17.9	22.9	53.0	61.4	86.2	78.9	920
18.3	32.4	16.4	19.6	49.9	57.3	89.5	85.6	750
42.3	51.1	30.5	38.4	69.0	66.3	78.8	42.8	11,390
36.1	53.7	17.7	20.7	52.6	59.1	83.0	84.6	690
18.2	28.3	17.4	20.8	54.1	60.0	83.6	79.5	860
36.0	49.9	17.9	20.9	53.3	58.8	94.8	59.1	NA
42.6	60.7	19.4	25.4	55.8	64.2	71.2	23.6	1,880
12.8	20.6	15.3	18.1	48.2	54.9	86.3	80.0	920
25.0	38.7	17.5	21.8	52.6	61.0	90.1	86.1	1,200
35.2	44.7	16.9	20.3	51.4	59.2	91.0	66.0	1,220
36.8	50.7	19.0	24.5	57.0	64.8	84.7	64.1	NA
55.8	71.6	16.6	18.8	51.2	55.5	91.5	73.7	4,400
56.0	71.0	18.7	24.2	54.7	63.9	79.9	51.8	2,120
38.4	48.4	18.3	22.2	53.5	61.3	89.4	70.5	740
26.1	41.2	16.8	19.3	50.8	56.3	77.5	65.9	1,280
60.9	70.9	18.8	23.2	54.9	62.9	87.7	56.8	2,750
33.3	49.2	16.3	17.7	50.2	53.7	90.6	61.4	290
84.7	90.6	21.5	28.0	59.4	65.9	83.3	61.8	13,080
58.9	72.7	21.1	26.5	61.1	66.4	69.6	45.9	12,420
24.7	42.4	18.8	22.6	54.9	61.7	73.5	46.1	1,890
36.2	51.5	19.5	25.3	57.4	64.5	62.8	46.5	512
60.2	71.3	23.9	27.7	63.6	65.7	79.2	45.8	9,560
24.6	37.0	18.9	22.3	57.0	62.1	74.8	31.9	4,930
40.8	53.7	17.7	21.9	53.1	60.4	86.1	53.6	1,310
19.1	32.6	16.8	20.3	50.7	58.5	89.4	77.6	1,120
48.2	62.8	18.5	24.0	55.1	63.7	88.7	38.8	1,590
55.7	71.0	19.5	24.1	55.1	61.9	86.1	59.0	1,140
49.3	64.7	19.9	26.3	57.4	65.1	75.3	70.3	1,330
33.9	48.6	18.1	20.9	53.6	60.0	87.4	79.7	1,120
29.7	38.6	16.2	17.2	49.5	52.4	92.6	61.1	470
59.5	73.7	16.4	17.5	50.9	53.3	83.4	54.5	290
31.6	47.4	16.0	18.9	48.7	55.9	82.3	72.0	1,040
40.7	51.7	19.6	25.5	56.1	64.3	84.2	54.4	2,010
16.4	23.7	16.0	17.5	48.9	51.4	95.1	70.9	630
47.6	63.6	17.6	22.4	52.7	61.7	85.2	45.5	1,770
42.0	53.2	18.5	24.2	53.6	63.2	81.0	55.6	1,640
37.4	49.0	18.5	19.7	53.9	56.7	94.2	56.1	660
41.3	57.3	18.1	23.5	53.7	62.9	89.9	50.3	800